Overcoming Common P

How to Cope with Stress
DR PETER TYRER

How to Cope with your Child's Allergies
DR PAUL CARSON

How to Cope with your Nerves
DR TONY LAKE

How to Cope with Tinnitus and Hearing Loss
DR ROBERT YOUNGSON

How to Do What You Want to Do
DR PAUL HAUCK

How to Enjoy Your Old Age
DR B. F. SKINNER AND M. E.
VAUGHAN

How to Interview and Be Interviewed
MICHELE BROWN AND
GYLES BRANDRETH

How to Improve Your Confidence
DR KENNETH HAMBLY

How to Love a Difficult Man
NANCY GOOD

How to Love and be Loved
DR PAUL HAUCK

How to Say No to Alcohol
KEITH McNEILL

How to Sleep Better
DR PETER TYRER

How to Stand up for Yourself
DR PAUL HAUCK

How to Start a Conversation and Make Friends
DON GABOR

How to Stop Feeling Guilty
DR VERNON COLEMAN

How to Stop Smoking
GEORGE TARGET

How to Stop Taking Tranquillisers
DR PETER TYRER

If Your Child is Diabetic
JOANNE ELLIOTT

Jea
DR

Le
DF
Al

Liv
DR TONY LAKE

Living Through Personal Crisis
ANN KAISER STEARNS

Living with High Blood Pressure
DR TOM SMITH

Loneliness
DR TONY LAKE

Making Marriage Work
DR PAUL HAUCK

Making the Most of Loving
GILL COX AND SHEILA DAINOW

Making the Most of Yourself
GILL COX AND SHEILA DAINOW

Making Relationships Work
CHRISTINE SANDFORD AND WYN
BEARDSLEY

Meeting People is Fun
How to overcome shyness
DR PHYLLIS SHAW

One Parent Families
DIANA DAVENPORT

Overcoming Fears and Phobias
DR TONY WHITEHEAD

Overcoming Stress
DR VERNON COLEMAN

Overcoming Tension
DR KENNETH HAMBLY

The Parkinson's Disease Handbook
DR RICHARD GODWIN-AUSTEN

Second Wife, Second Best?
Managing your marriage as a second wife
GLYNNIS WALKER

Self-Help for your Arthritis
EDNA PEMBLE

Overcoming Common Problems Series

Overcoming Common Problems

COPING SUCCESSFULLY WITH YOUR CHILD'S SKIN PROBLEMS

Dr Paul Carson

SHELDON PRESS
LONDON

First published in Great Britain in 1988 by
Sheldon Press, SPCK, Marylebone Road, London NW1 4DU

British Library Cataloguing in Publication Data

Carson, Paul, *1949–*
    Coping successfully with your child's
    skin problems.
    1. Children. Skin. Diseases
    I. Title   II. Series
    618.92'5

    ISBN 0–85969–569–7

Photoset by Deltatype Ltd, Ellesmere Port, South Wirral
Printed in Great Britain by Biddles Ltd, Guildford, Surrey

*For every child who has had to scratch but rather
wished they didn't need to!*

*But especially for Karen Murphy and Daíre McNab
who don't itch so much any more.*

Contents

Acknowledgements

Many people have helped, both directly and indirectly, in the research for this book. Among those who have made the greatest contributions are Dr P. J. August, Consultant Dermatologist, the Skin Hospital, Manchester, England; Dr Sarah Rogers, Consultant Dermatologist, Hume St and St Vincent's Hospitals, Dublin, Ireland; Wendy Lyons, nurse in charge, Burns Unit, Dunedin Hospital, New Zealand; and Dr Philip Hopkins, London, England, who has pioneered the technique of cryosurgery in Britain and instructed me in its use. My thanks are due to them for their time and patience with my queries. I am particularly indebted to Dr David Atherton, Paediatric Dermatologist, Gt Ormond St Hospital, London, England; and Prof. Ronald Vickers, Consultant Dermatologist, Alder Hey Children's Hospital, Liverpool, England, who allowed me to join their busy hospital clinics and listen in on the advice they give on a variety of conditions, particularly eczema: this book contains some fairly new and, perhaps, controversial ideas on the management of atopic eczema, but they are well thought through and quite sensible.

A particularly important contribution to this book has been made by the children who attend my practice. To them I am grateful for the wealth of experience I have gained and to which I am adding every day – life would not be the same without them!

Last, but by no means least, I am especially grateful to Miss Lesley Allen, typist, receptionist, coffee-maker supreme, and decipherer of my worst scribbles!

Introduction

'Doctor, – is that rash infectious?' 'Is it harmful?' 'Is that cream too strong for the face?' 'Is there cortisone in it?' The seemingly endless queries of parents to doctors about their children's skin problems are a reflection of how complicated and confusing life is becoming nowadays. With an increasing media attention on health-related topics a lot of (often contradictory) information has to be assessed carefully so that the practical application of this knowledge is correct. Nowhere is this more important than when dealing with children's problems. Whatever medical decisions we take upon ourselves as adults at least we can usually tell quite quickly whether the results are good, bad or indifferent. However, children may not have the vocabulary or insight to tell directly that they are feeling better or worse than before the treatment began. Consequently any decisions you make on your child's behalf concerning health matters should be sensibly thought through in combination with your doctor's advice.

This book deals with the most common skin problems that children are likely to experience from birth to mid-teens. Skin problems are an important part of the daily workload of most family doctors and range from trivial insect bites, where reassurance is the only treatment, through to atopic eczema, the management of which is time-consuming, tedious and often frustratingly complicated. However, in the rush of a busy surgery many parents find their questions about condition and treatment go unanswered.

This book will help you understand better what type of skin problem your child has, why it occurred in the first place, and the forms of treatment that are available. You can read about the correct use of creams, pastes, lotions and ointments so that you have a clearer idea about how and why they are chosen. In particular, you can learn about the cortisone-based preparations – so very widely used nowadays – and understand which type is likely to be useful in your child's condition when needed. I will also draw your attention to the side-effects you should keep an eye out for in any treatment. In addition I have listed the most commonly prescribed medications and preparations, with guidelines on how much, how often and for how long they are likely to be used.

Use this book as a ready reference guide – find out (from your doctor) the exact name of the condition your child has and go straight to

1

the page dealing with it in Chapter 2. There you will find details of causes, treatment and a likely time-scale of management. Next, consult Chapter 3 for details of treatments – the types of medication used, their strengths and potential side-effects. Armed with this information you will have a better idea on the progress of the skin blemish from eruption to resolution.

Do, please, read all of Chapter 1, which explains how your child's skin lives and breathes, so that you will have a clearer understanding of what is happening during eruption of rash (or whatever) and spontaneous or medically-induced clearing. This chapter also explains some of the complicated-sounding medical jargon you are likely to come up against from doctors and chemists. Once you realize that such jargon is no more than a smoke-screen to keep non-doctors in ignorance of medical matters you will become more interested in penetrating the camouflage. Don't be put off by long-winded Latin names – they are no more than labels, tags which set apart one different rash from another.

Finally, you will find more attention paid to the stubborn, difficult conditions such as eczema and psoriasis. I trust you will understand that these complicated and time-consuming problems deserve more detail. Hopefully you will still find this book a ready guide and reference source for whatever skin blemish your child has – even if it is only a mild nappy rash.

1

Your child's skin

Skin function

No doubt you are aware of the heart, lung and liver transplants that have been carried out around the world in recent years? Collectively these operations are known as organ transplants – the word *organ* refers to the individual parts of the body transferred from one individual (the donor) to another (the recipient). An organ is a distinct structure which has a specific function in the body. For example, the heart pumps blood around the body, the lungs transfer oxygen to the blood and the kidneys filter and excrete some of the waste products from daily body functions. These are all separate organs, totally dependent upon one another for their individual existences. If the heart stops pumping then the lungs and kidneys will cease to function as well. Equally, if the kidneys stop working then all other organs are affected by the subsequent accumulation of waste products to the point where they too cease to perform.

In a very roundabout way this leads me to the organ we are most concerned with in this book – the skin, and in particular your child's skin. However, the lead-up should help you grasp a most important point – all organs are more or less dependent on one another. Your child's skin is almost as important a structure as his or her liver or lungs or heart. However, the skin, being very much an 'outside' organ, is in many ways the body's first line of defence, and there are many more common skin problems than there are common inside-organ problems.

The skin has several important functions:

- It regulates body temperature by opening pores to cause sweating when the body is too warm, and closing pores to prevent heat loss in cold conditions.
- It gets rid of some of the waste products of daily living.
- It acts as an organ of sensation so that we are totally aware of our immediate environment; for example, it enables us to feel heat and cold, wet and dry, and so on.
- It acts as a barrier against infection by covering the body with a protective scale.
- It protects against excessive sunburning by producing pigment in response to sun exposure.
- It manufactures some of the vitamin D we need every day.

The diagram below shows what your child's skin looks like under a microscope. As you can see, it is composed of separate layers. Each of these has its own function. Through these layers run various sweat glands, hair follicles and blood vessels. An understanding of these functions will help you to grasp the treatment routines explained in Chapter 2. Don't be frightened by the strange names in the diagram, nor indeed of any of the technical terms used in this book: they will be explained for you where necessary, and many are listed in Appendix 7.

The *scaly layer* is the outermost layer of your child's skin – the surface. It is composed of a tough dry scale, which acts as a barrier. *The epidermis* is a firm, slightly deeper, layer of cells which is constantly active. At the bottom of the epidermis new cells are formed which migrate towards the surface, becoming more scaly as they progress. At the surface they shed.

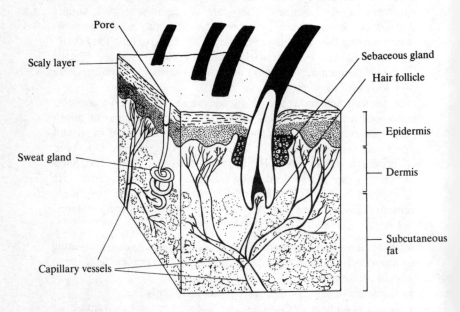

Beneath the epidermis is the *dermis*, a thicker, tougher layer of skin which contains a fine mesh of minute blood vessels, called *capillaries*, which enable the skin to function properly, and the nerves which supply sensation to the skin, enabling us, for example, to be aware of pain or discomfort.

The dermis also contains the 'roots' or *follicles* from which body hairs arise; these follicles are responsible for the growth of these hairs. At

4

this skin level also are the *sebaceous glands*, which are associated with the hair follicles. These glands produce a greasy material called *sebum*. They are very small in children, and become functional only at puberty, when they may become temporarily overactive, causing acne. (If you have ever squeezed a pimple on your face you will know what sebum is – the white cheesy material inside the pimple.)

Still in the dermis, here are also the *sweat glands*. The body has a rich supply of these, and some areas, such as under the armpits, have more than others. Each of these is connected to the skin surface by a tube; at the end of this is a *pore*. The network of pores all over the body act as a temperature-regulating mechanism, opening to allow moisture to escape to keep us cool, or closing when we need to keep warm.

Lastly, underneath the dermis is a layer of fatty tissue, or *subcutaneous* fat, which gives skin its 'spongy' feel.

As you can see, your child's skin is a very important organ, capable of 'breathing' via the pores and acting as a protective barrier against infection The outer scaly layer, when intact, is an excellent shield for the body. It is only when that outer surface becomes broken (for whatever reason) that many problems occur.

How and why your child's skin becomes damaged or diseased

For every child the journey from inside the protection of mother's womb to the outside world is a traumatic event. The first gasps of air and convulsive cries herald the beginning of the infant's adjustment to his new environment. Lungs are exposed to dust and smoke and other air contaminants, while the intestines experience a totally different, perhaps even artificial, form of food. The child's body has to adapt to these new sensations and stimuli. However, once the trauma of birth is over, the baby soon settles, and comes to terms with the outside world – provided that a safe, warm and protective environment exists.

Three organs come into immediate contact with the outside world after birth in a way which will determine the growing child's health for the rest of his life: the lungs ('new' air is inhaled for the first time); the intestines ('new' food is experienced for the first time); and the skin (the beginning of handling, rubbing, cleaning, wetting, drying, and so on, from birth to death).

As the child's skin adjusts to this environment all sorts of adverse factors conspire to interfere with the strong protective scaly barrier nature has developed. It is how that protective barrier fails to cope and the reasons behind this breakdown that concern us now.

The first possible problem to arise in small children and babies is *inflammation* from either internal or external causes. This implies that the child's skin blisters, weeps, itches and becomes reddened, as in nappy rash where urine-soaked nappies irritate the soft sensitive skin of small infants causing the surface to break down. The next possible problem is caused by direct skin damage, as in cuts and burns, which break the protective outer skin barrier. After these, *infections* are the most likely problems – however, in the majority of cases infections can only become a nuisance when the infecting 'bugs' settle on broken skin, where the protective barrier is breached, allowing bugs to feed off the underlying, more nourishing tissue. For example, if a child becomes burned and the skin blisters, then the exposed lower skin is a rich source of food for passing 'bugs' which will quickly invade and multiply if left unchecked.

These are the 'big three' causes of skin disorder in small children, although as the years progress other problems may occur some of which are relatively minor, such as warts, or quite troublesome, such as psoriasis.

As children grow older other problems also arise. If we look at all age groups – from infancy to mid-teens, then the following list contains the most frequently encountered skin disorders for which medical attention is sought:

- *Inflammation*, which is a break in skin continuity, with redness, itching and weeping. This may be due to *external* causes, such as nappy rash, or *internal* causes, such as atopic eczema, which can be caused by a food allergy.
- *Infection*, which may be due, most commonly, to *bacteria* or *viruses*, or occasionally, to *fungi* and *yeasts*.
- *Direct or indirect damage*, as occurs, for example, in scalding by hot liquids or in sunburn.
- *Infestations*, where small insects invade the hairy skin areas, settle there and lay eggs. Scabies is an example of this type of problem.
- *Excessive drying and scaling of skin*, as in dandruff.
- *Excessive sweating*.
- *Pigmentation changes*, where white areas appear on the surface of the skin.
- *Alopecia*, or hair loss.
- *Ulceration*, which is a distinct breakdown in skin structure.
- *Miscellaneous lumps and bumps*.

Inflammation

Inflammation (called *dermatitis* or *eczema*) is the commonest skin problem in children. Leaving aside whatever causes the reaction in the first place, the skin changes are fairly consistent with disruption in the layers of dermis and epidmermis (look again at the diagram on page 4). Blood cells, which are not usually present in these tissues, move in and release chemicals that irritate the skin cells causing itch, redness and scratching. As the skin is scratched a further irritation with more redness and itching develops. In addition the affected skin swells and begins to ooze fluid. The skin is inflamed. If the cause is not removed and the skin allowed to heal, either on its own or with the use of medication, then an itch–scratch cycle becomes established leading to a prolonged condition (called *chronic eczema*).

In general, the long-standing eczema condition develops in three separate stages as follows:

- Stage 1 – the acute (or immediate) reaction. The skin becomes red, itchy, swollen and 'bubbly' at the surface. The bubbles are called *blisters* and they eventually burst and weep a clear fluid.
- Stage 2 – the secondary reaction. The skin is less swollen and there is less blistering or weeping. However, redness, scaling and itching are still present. Persistent itching leads to persisting scratching which aggravates and perpetuates an itch–scratch cycle. This must be broken if the skin is to heal.
- Stage 3 – the chronic or 'long drawn-out' stage. This stage is really the end result of constantly itchy skin. As the surface is repeatedly rubbed away by scratching the skin becomes thickened, raised and excessively scaly. It looks decidedly unhealthy and irritable.

In some forms of childhood eczema all three stages of inflammation can be present at any one time on different areas of the child's body. This reflects how the condition is constantly bubbling away, erupting every now and then with fresh vigour.

When inflamed skin is in the first or second stages then the removal of the underlying cause may be all that is needed to produce healing – provided the damaged area does not become infected and is allowed enough air. A quicker method of restoring the normal skin surface is to use one of the cortisone creams (these will crop up repeatedly in Chapter 2 and their use is explained in Appendix 1). If your child's skin has reached stage 3 then it will not heal very well on its own and really needs proper management using cortisone creams in a 'sliding scale' (see Appendix 1).

Cortisone creams (or *steroid* creams, as they are also called) have an anti-inflammatory effect – they reduce inflammation. For this reason they are widely used to treat eczema and are very, very successful.

When sensibly and correctly prescribed they are completely safe, produce an excellent clearing of damaged skin and speed up the recovery phase.

Infection

If you recall the diagram at the beginning of this chapter you will remember that skin is composed of different layers. The outer scaly layer is a protective barrier and prevents infection in the tissue beneath it. This is because the scale is dry and constantly being shed. Infecting 'bugs' need more than this to sustain growth and so rarely get a hold on healthy skin. When this shield is broken – for whatever reason – then the infecting bugs can penetrate to the deeper skin tissue where the environment is much more to their liking.

The usual causes of the scaly shield layer becoming broken are:

- *direct damage*, as from cuts and bruises.
- *indirect damage*, as from sunburn, causing peeling and blistering of skin.
- *an underlying inflammation* from whatever source – as I have just explained, inflamed skin usually leads to a breakdown in the normal surface.

As soon as the barrier is broken there is the potential for infection. For that reason broken skin should be kept clean and dry and wiped initially with an antiseptic. If an infection does develop then it may be *localized* to the immediate damaged area or *spread* to other areas. Localized infections are usually treated with regular antiseptic cleansers or local antibiotic (bacteria-killing) creams. If the infection has spread further than the damaged skin then antibiotics must be taken internally (usually as pills) so that the bloodstream carries the drug to the infected areas and kills the 'bugs'. Clues to look out for which suggest an infection has spread are:

- A red line stretching from the damaged skin to the nearest glands, for example, in the armpit or groin.
- Pain in the affected areas.
- Swollen, tender glands.
- Fever.

When the infection clears the underlying skin can begin to heal. It will *never* heal while actively infected.

Treatment of infections varies according to whether they are caused by bacteria, fungi or viruses. Bacterial infections are treated by antiseptics or antibiotic creams, if the infection is localized, or by taking antibiotic tablets, if it has spread. Fungal and yeast infections are treated in a similar way: creams for localized infections, tablets for more generalized infections. Viral infections produce a wider range of problems than do bacteria. For example, cold sores on the lips are caused by one specific virus while common hand warts are caused by a different virus altogether. Because of the complexity of the treatments used in viral infections I will deal with them individually as they arise in Chapter 2.

Skin damage from outside sources

It is very common for a child's skin to be damaged from the direct effects of falling, cutting or burning. A fall onto the knee may peel away the outer skin layers and leave bleeding, sore tissue exposed. If that damaged area is not too large and is kept clean then nature will produce all the healing that is necessary – no medication is needed. However if bits of gravel or dirt are left in the grazed area then infection will almost certainly set in and require treatment. So the first rule of thumb in cuts and grazes is: *clean the damaged area thoroughly with an antiseptic solution.* If the graze is kept clean no further interference will be necessary.

If your child falls onto broken glass and cuts himself badly then a different approach should be adopted. First, the cut must be thoroughly cleaned – healing cannot occur in a dirty wound. Then the two edges of the cut skin are pulled together so that the wound is not gaping open. For some deep cuts this may mean having stitches inserted for a few days to keep the separated tissues held together. This promotes a quicker, cleaner and more solid healing. Also, the raw edges, if kept together, are not exposed to passing bacteria which would find such tissue ideal for growth.

Depending on how deep the cut is, perhaps only one type of stitch will be used. However, for very deep wounds a totally absorbable cat-gut stitch is inserted into the deeper tissue to keep it together and then an ordinary (but totally sterile) silk thread stitch pulls the top layers into place again. The deeper cat-gut stitches dissolve long after they have ceased to be effective, while the silk stitches need to be cut and pulled out from the wound. This is an almost pain-free procedure.

Burns to your child's skin are much more serious and potentially more damaging than the above and for this reason special attention is always required. In Chapter 2 I have set out specific guidelines on the correct management of all types of burns including sunburn.

Other causes

The other causes of childhood skin problems, such as infestations, pigment changes, along with their proper managements are dealt with individually in Chapter 2.

Medical jargon

When I first entered medical school I found myself totally out of depth in a world of strange-sounding names and equally unusual study subjects. For the first year I floundered, trying hard not to show my ignorance every time a new medical word was thrown at me. Mandible, nephritis, cerebellum, duodenum, tracheotomy – the terms just seemed to keep coming, thick and fast, and I had to sneak a peek into my well-worn nursing dictionary to keep up. As the years progressed and I mastered this new language I, too, began to spout out terms and phrases which meant little to anyone but myself and my colleagues. They most certainly meant nothing to the people I was supposed to be communicating with – my patients.

When you take your child to the doctor (or, even more seriously, to hospital and the skin specialist there) you are likely to come up against the same problem as I found at medical school: strange labels and terms, meant to communicate explanations but serving only to reinforce the confusion. To help you understand more clearly what doctors, nurses, chemists and other medical workers actually mean when they talk about your child's skin problems I have compiled a short list of terms, and their explanation. Have a quick read through them so that you will understand better some of the medical jargon you might encounter in the rest of this book or when you visit the doctor. A more comprehensive list is contained in Appendix 7.

dermatologist	A doctor who specializes in skin problems.
paediatric dermatologist	A doctor who specializes in the skin problems of children.
eczema, dermatitis	Two different labels which mean the same: an inflammation of the skin.
cortisone, steroid	Two different labels which mean the same: a drug which occurs naturally in the body but which also can be given in various forms – creams, ointments, tablets and injections – to reduce inflammation wherever it occurs.
macule	A discoloration (usually red) of the skin, but not raised up on the skin's surface.
papule	An 'above-the-surface' discoloration of skin, as occurs in chickenpox.

vesicle	A small blister containing clear fluid. These may be scattered irregularly over the skin, as in chicken-pox, or grouped in clusters, as in cold sores (see Chapter 2).
pustule	A blister containing pus, usually meaning an infection is present.
crust	A scab-type formation found on inflamed skin.
weal	A localized swelling of the skin which is usually white or pinkish-white with a surrounding redness. Weals vary in size and never burst; they are characteristic of allergy.
erythema	Redness of the skin.
petechia	A small bleed under the surface of the skin.
ecchymosis	A large bleed under the skin surface. (You and I call these *bruises*!)
comedone	A 'blackhead', as present in acne.
nodule	A localized thickening of the skin.
cyst	A balloon-like collection of cheesy material found under the skin surface.
lesion	Any type of skin blemish.

These are the terms most frequently encountered in skin disorders and will give you a working knowledge of what your doctor is talking about when next you visit with any form of skin blemish on yourself or your child.

Before finishing this chapter I want to remind you again of the close relationship between all body organs. Your child's skin will reflect any underlying medical condition and may give your doctor important clues as to what is happening inside the body. For example, if your child is anaemic (that is, has a low red blood-cell count) then he/she may look pale and have an unusually whitish skin generally. If your child has some forms of kidney disease there may be an unusual lemon-yellow tinge to the skin generally. If your child has a bad infection inside the body the skin will be moist, unusually suffused and feel hot to the touch.

The next chapter is an A–Z listing of the common skin conditions experienced by children. Now that you know something of how your child's skin works, what it does, how it can be damaged or diseased, and now that you know what some of the technical terms which doctors use actually mean, you should find Chapter 2 quite easy to use.

Throughout this book you will read of medicines such as antibiotics, anti-fungals, cortisone, moisturizers, antiseptics, etc. You may wish to use some of these on your child but find that your chemist will insist you see a doctor for a prescription. In general terms the following preparations can only be obtained by prescription – antibiotics, anti-fungals, antihistamines, psoriasis treatments. All cortisone/steroid preparations are available only on prescription, except for hydrocortisone 1% creams/ointments, which are now non-prescription items in Britain.

Available in any good pharmacy, without a prescription, are moisturizers, antiseptics, most wart-killing preparations, all anti-infestation preparations and many anti-acne skin preparations.

2

Common Skin Problems:
From Acne to Warts

This chapter deals with the most common skin problems that occur in children. Rare or exotic conditions will not be included as this would make the book both complicated and unbalanced. I refer to various specific treatments, and I mention if they are only available on prescription. The others can be bought across the counter in any good pharmacy. The antibiotics mentioned are only available on prescription. Words in **bold italic type** are explained in more detail elsewhere in this chapter.

Acne vulgaris

This is the bane of teenagers everywhere! Many anxious hours are spent in front of mirrors watching the latest crop of pimples erupt and despairing that life is so hard on the eve of a 'big date'. Ignore the vulgaris part of the descriptive label – it merely means 'common', not vulgar as you might have thought! Acne is the medical term given to the pimples, spots and bumps which commonly erupt on the face, shoulders, chest and back of teenagers. Males are more prone to the condition than females and the worst years are between 14 and 17.

The main problem in acne begins with those sebaceous glands you read about in Chapter 1. These secrete an oily material called *sebum* whose function is to soften and lubricate the skin. During adolescence, under the influence of hormones, these glands often become overproductive so that sebum is poured out from the hair follicle on to the skin surface, resulting in the face becoming shiny with oil. What happens in acne is that the outlet of the gland, the skin pore, becomes plugged with sebum at or near the skin surface to form blackheads or whiteheads.

In very mild cases of acne, nothing more may happen. In most other cases, the plug of sebum in the hair follicle is broken down by the action of bacteria so that it may eventually burst or seep into the surrounding skin and cause inflammation. The end result can often be the formation of solid red bumps, spots or pimples or even large fluid-containing swellings called *cysts*.

Acne tends to begin in the teenage years and can persist into the late 20s if not managed properly. Because the spots are in the visibly obvious area of the face, the condition can cause marked psychological problems. In the more severe forms of acne the facial features are actually distorted by cysts and in such cases recent treatments have much to offer.

There are three broad types of acne which I shall label *mild*, *moderate* and *severe* for the sake of simplicity. The mild form involves persisting blackheads (which doctors call *comedones*) and red pimples affecting mainly the face. The areas on the face most troubled are the chin and forehead.

Moderate acne is more troublesome in that the sufferer tends to have quite greasy skin with the spots covering the face, chest and back. Quite often the comedones go on to become the red, throbbing pimples which are the hallmark of acne.

Severe acne means exactly that. In addition to the comedones and pimples there are cysts, hard nodules and often scarring. The cysts are full of sebum but occasionally become infected and then contain pus as well. The cysts may discharge from one or more different points onto the skin surface.

Scarring often follows acne and depends on the depth and intensity of inflammation in the skin. Some people seem to be more vulnerable to scar formation than others and occasionally the scars can be deep and thick.

The causes of acne are many and diverse. Inheritance is important –if one or both parents had bad acne then that does increase the chance of the teenage children having similar problems. Diet – despite doctors' dismissal of the suggestion – is important in some cases. Climate also has a part to play – acne is much less troublesome in sunny countries. Hormone changes are also important and it is no coincidence that acne erupts after puberty and it can also be treated by some types of artificial hormone therapies.

One last point to note is that bacteria can settle on areas affected by acne, leading, as you will understand if you've read Chapter 1, to infections.

In managing the condition, there are a few important general guidelines which many acne sufferers ignore or are unaware of and which go a long way towards keeping the condition manageable.

- *Diet*. Certain foods, particularly chocolate derivatives, sugary products, nuts, ice-creams and health foods such as kelp tablets aggravate the problem. Greasy foods, and particularly junk foods, are probably best avoided.
- *Cleaning*. Always wash the face with a simple, *non-scented* soap at least twice daily. The hair should be shampooed three times each week.

- *To squeeze or not to squeeze.* No matter what guidelines are issued here people tend to do their own thing anyway. If the blackheads or pimples are to be squeezed then make sure the hands are well scrubbed before and that clean cotton wool is used. It is a good idea to soften the skin and 'loosen' the sebum with a hot flannel in advance. The skin should be carefully washed and patted dry afterwards.

- *Medical treatments should not be abandoned before the recommended time.* Some treatments will not begin to show results for months but should be long-lasting.

- *Don't waste money* on the silly 'over-the-counter' preparations widely advertised. They generally are of little use in established acne.

For all mild and some moderate forms of acne the applications of certain creams onto the affected skin will work wonders. The single most useful group contain a preparation called *benzoyl peroxide* in various concentrations. For most people a 5% concentration in a gel form is all that is necessary. The entire face, chest or back should be treated, as the primary aim is to prevent fresh spots erupting. The frequency of application is varied until the skin becomes slightly dry or an improvement is noticed. If the acne is more troublesome, it will require benzoyl peroxide combined with an antibiotic cream (to kill off the bacteria which invade the acne spots).

Acne which fails to respond to these measures will require a more aggressive approach. This invariably involves the use of long-term antibiotics in small doses. The dosage is enough to kill off the 'bugs' involved in acne but not so strong as to interfere with good health. The improvement of the condition in people using this approach is very satisfactory and most failures are due to not following the doctor's instructions or stopping treatment too early. The main antibiotic group used here is known as *tetracycline* and *must* be taken on an empty stomach. If the drug is taken at mealtimes, it will be prevented from being absorbed and will be ineffective.

Occasionally the tetracyclines do not work, and this may be because the 'bugs' are resistant. This means that the bacteria involved in acne will not be killed off by these particular antibiotics and a different type of antibiotic will be needed. This will probably be one of the *erythromycin* type (see Appendix 2). If you are changed to one of these do remember to take them correctly and for the length of time they are prescribed – usually a minimum of three months.

Severe acne may require a more specialized treatment and a new drug called *Roaccutane* is held in reserve for this situation. I must stress that it is used only as a *last* resort and when all other treatments have been shown to fail and is available only from skin specialists. Roaccutane causes drying of the skin and tissues everywhere allowing people with greasy, oily skin to find a new texture within weeks of treatment. Unfortunately because all tissue is dried up some unpleasant effects are found elsewhere such as dry, gritty eyes and sore lips. The results from using Roaccutane are very impressive and have allowed many people blighted with acne to literally show their faces again in society. However, because it still is a new drug and has many side-effects, especially if there is any risk of pregnancy, it may be some time before it becomes freely available.

In some girls with troublesome acne a form of hormonal treatment is very useful as it decreases sebum production. The hormone used is called *cyproterone* but will be prescribed in its more usual name, Diane. This treatment has a contraceptive effect and will regulate periods. The tablet is taken daily for 21 days starting on the fifth day of the menstrual cycle. Treatment lasts for several months.

In small babies a form of infantile acne can develop, almost certainly as a response to the mother's hormones still circulating in the child. It requires no treatment and resolves quickly in the majority of cases .

Alopecia

This is the medical term for localized or generalized loss of hair leading to balding. From the time of birth the hair follicles in the scalp are in a continuous cycle of growth and shedding. This pattern is very complicated and can be upset by many different internal and external factors. In general, about 100 hairs are shed and replaced each day. The average head has around 100,000 hairs, with blonds having more than redheads.

Alopecia areata is the usual type of balding seen in children and can occur at any age from around five years upwards. It is no respecter of class or sex and frequently occurs without warning. The first patch is usually round or oval-shaped and is totally devoid of hair. The skin of the affected area is usually quite normal, without any sign of scarring or inflammation. Occasionally there may be some slight itching and redness at the beginning. Often multiple patches may appear on the scalp, but sometimes the alopecia is confined to only one patch. In 5–10% of cases all scalp hair may be ultimately lost. In about 10% of cases sites other than the scalp – the hair of the eyelashes, eyebrows, or pubic or general body hair – may be affected. In a small percentage of cases the condition goes on to *alopecia universalis*, where all body and scalp hair is lost. In some cases of alopecia areata the nails may be affected, and show pitting, thickening and ridging of the nail plate.

The cause of alopecia is usually a total mystery but in a very small proportion of children some underlying condition may be implicated such as:

- a recent severe feverish illness;
- thyroid deficiency;
- iron deficiency in the blood;
- certain drug treatments;
- severe physical or emotional stress;
- pernicous anaemia (due to lack of vitamin B_{12});
- diabetes;
- a condition called Addison's disease – a very, very rare disease associated with a failure of the body's natural production of cortisone;
- perhaps (and only just perhaps) a link with *asthma* or *eczema*

In the majority of cases no real cause will ever be found and, while this is very frustrating, it is a fact that has to be understood and accepted.

The outcome in individual cases varies greatly but if the hair loss is confined to one or two areas of the scalp then the prospects for regrowth are good. However, recurrences can occur. In most cases the hair will grow back but you should be aware that the balding process may spread before it improves. Taking all cases together, the duration of the initial attack is less than six months in about a third of cases, less than a year in about half, and up to five years in three-quarters of cases. Approximately a fifth never recover at all from the initial hair loss, be it a large or small area.

Treatments are many and varied, and many of them are quite useless. It has been found, for example, that no vitamin or trace mineral supplements will make any difference to the recovery phase. *Cortisone* preparations, taken orally or by local injection into the bad patches, are favoured by some specialists and dismissed by others. My own feeling is that the only benefit to be gained is in being *seen* to be doing something while secretly knowing that success is unlikely. The oral route is unlikely to be tried in your child but local injections might be offered. This involves injecting 0.1 cc of a cortisone suspension into about four areas of the bald patch, repeated monthly for about four months. The usual response is after a few months a small tuft of hair grows at the site of the injection. If the process is resolving the tuft of hair will continue to grow and hair will grow spontaneously in the other patches. If the process is not settling the tuft of cortisone-induced hair will eventually fall out. It is an interesting phenomenon that the hair induced by injection is usually the normal colour of the patient's hair whereas the hair that grows spontaneously is at first depigmented and only afterwards assumes again the normal colour. If there is no response to this form of treatment after a couple of months the treatment should be stopped. Occasionally ultraviolet light treatment is offered on an out-patient basis, but its merits are dubious.

Most skin specialists asked about treatments for alopecia are in favour of allowing time to heal. Indeed, if the child has no underlying physical or emotional problem, time will do the trick. All the doctors questioned had tried different ideas over the years but rarely, if ever, had these produced any improvement. There is a new drug called *Minoxidil* (*Regaine* is the common trade name for it) which is used for the treatment of the kind of baldness seen in adult men. In all certainty it will also be tried in persisting childhood baldness but, as I write, there is no information on its effectiveness (or potential side-effect problems) in children. It is rubbed onto the head twice daily.

Finally, some children induce patchy baldness themselves by pulling at their hair so violently that the hair comes out, root and all. Bald patches erupt and will stay for as long as the child continues the practice. In these children occasionally an underlying psychological problem can be detected but, in my experience, many are perfectly normal and happy. When they eventually stop pulling their hair, it regrows to normal quality.

Angio-oedema. See *urticaria*.

Athlete's foot

This is the label commonly used for *tinea pedis*, a fungal infection of the toes and feet. It usually begins by not drying the web space between the toes properly, thus leaving the skin moist and eventually macerated. This is the ideal environment for fungi and yeasts, which quickly settle on the soggy skin and start to grow. The symptoms are itching, redness and often a breakdown of the skin. The fungi or yeasts are most often picked up in communal bathing places. The fungal infections can sometimes be fairly extensive, with large blistering affecting the sole, heel, toes and hands. To add insult to injury, bacteria can settle on top of the damaged skin. Where this is suspected an antiseptic or antibiotic preparation may be needed first to clear the infection off the skin as only then can the fungal element be dealt with. However, there are some creams available which kill both bacteria and fungi.

See *ringworm* for details on the treatment of the fungal elements of athlete's foot.

In practical terms if your child has had an episode of athlete's foot, then encourage changing of socks daily at least, careful drying between the toes after baths, showers or bathing in swimming pools. Where you have a child involved in regular sporting events then some form of rubber footwear should be worn in the shower areas and the feet and socks dusted with an anti-fungal powder.

Atopic eczema

Atopic eczema, also called *atopic dermatitis*, *infantile eczema* or just *eczema* is without a doubt one of the most perplexing and distressing of all the skin disorders affecting children. The condition is quite complicated, and so please bear with me as I try to explain how it occurs, why it occurs and how it is managed. Before you read any further may I stress that there are many opinions on both the causes and management of eczema, so what I will now suggest may not be everyone's cup of tea. However, this section is the result of a lot of research and personal discussion with many specialists in the field. The management routine given here is what I consider to be the most sensible, practical and useful regime available. It is a shameless poach of all the best ideas from these various skin specialists and is presented to you now in a 'treatment package'.

Atopic eczema is an allergic skin condition – *atopic* means allergic, *eczema* means inflammation, so the term implies an inflammation of the skin due to allergy. It is beyond the scope of this book to discuss all the ins and outs of allergy, but a few basic explanations are important if you are to understand the causes and treatments of atopic eczema. In addition you should read carefully Chapter 1, where I explain the features of skin inflammation and its management.

Let us look at allergy first. An allergic reaction occuring anywhere in the body, for example hay fever, in the eyes during the pollen season, produces an inflammation of the affected tissue – the tissue swells, itches and produces a blistering fluid ooze. Here the eyes are the affected tissue: pollen grains hit the lining of the eye and cause it to swell, itch and become very watery. This allergic reaction occurs to substances (in this case grass pollen) in the atmosphere and carried by air currents. The reaction is immediate and confined to the area where the pollen grains land – the eyes. However, a similar reaction can occur if you consume a food or drink to which you are allergic. In this case the response may occur locally (in the stomach or intestines) or at a distance from the initial reaction. For example some people develop headaches after eating chocolate – the reaction occurs in the gut but the end response is in the brain. In allergy conditions the main types of reaction occur in response to something consumed, inhaled or which comes into direct contact with the skin.

Examples of these three allergy responses are:

(a) migraine brought on by eating chocolate
(b) asthma brought on by inhaling pollen
(c) skin inflammation from handling certain materials.

This may seem complicated, but if you can grasp these important points then the rest of this section will make more sense. Atopic eczema is probably brought on by an allergy to something consumed, but in many chronic (long-lasting) cases it may be kept simmering by allergy reactions to substances inhaled or coming into direct contact with the already inflamed skin. In some individuals all three mechanisms may conspire together to keep the eczema roaring away.

Atopic eczema ranges from mild, episodic patches of redness and itch on the skin through to a chronic, dry, scaly, red, itchy and unhealthy looking skin. It is largely a children's disease, and as many as 5% of children suffer from it. Three quarters of all children with eczema develop it in the first year of life. Most commonly the baby has good skin until about three or four months of age, when an irritating rash starts to develop in the face, worsens quickly and leaves the cheeks raw and weeping. The rash may appear elsewhere but the face is usually the worst affected area. The baby may continually rub its face against the bedclothes for relief from the itch. This stage may settle and disappear or it may gradually turn into a more established form. If it persists it tends to progress onto the body, arms and legs eventually settling in the creases of the elbows, wrists, buttocks, knees and ankles.

The severe forms of eczema are dreadfully distressing, leaving the affected child and his or her parents drained and irritable all the time. So troublesome can the condition become that occasionally one or other of the parents snaps totally and tries to end the misery in a fairly dramatic way – by smothering the child! In a recent study (following a much publicized court case dealing with a mother who killed her child, who was severely affected with eczema) three out of the first 250 parents attending the out-patients department of a skin hospital admitted to having seriously tried a similar solution, backing off only at the last moment.

One of the perplexing features of eczema is its tendency to fluctuate wildly in severity and to erupt for no obvious reason. The hallmark of the condition is its intense itch and some children will sit in a semi-hypnotic state tearing at their skin, doing dreadful damage that takes days to heal.

As I have already stated, atopic eczema is an allergy problem, and indeed the skin may be only one of many organs affected by the allergy. For example many affected children have problems affecting the eyes (conjunctivitis), nose (rhinitis), chest (asthma), brain (recurring headaches), joints (pain), and bowel (recurring pain, occasionally other more dramatic symptoms). While we are concentrating on the skin component in this book the other allergy problems mentioned above are dealt with in my other books: *How To Cope With Your Child's Allergies*, *Coping Successfully With Your Child's Asthma*, and *Coping Successfully With Your Hyperactive Child*, also published by Sheldon Press.

I will now explain in as simple terms as are practical what possibly happens to produce atopic eczema in the first place and what keeps it going in the long-term cases.

With babies the initial cause of the allergic reaction is usually food – this means that something the child digests can cause an allergic reaction in the body. This can occur to both breast- and bottle-fed babies – breast milk carries the same protein foods to the child that the mother is eating and drinking. The allergic reaction occurs in the child's intestines causing the release of various chemicals which can irritate the body. For example, many milk-allergic babies have colic – the allergic reaction occurs in the bowel. In some unfortunate children the chemicals released during the allergic process travel to the skin and cause inflammation (see Chapter 1 for details on what this means) with a resulting itch, redness and breakdown of the skin surface.

As the child becomes older he or she will come into contact with other allergy-provoking substances, which influence the condition. The main offenders in the regard are:

House dust mites: microscopic insects which live in and feed off household dust, but have a special fancy for human skin scales. For this reason house dust mites are found mainly in beds and bedrooms as we tend to naturally shed our outer skin layers more freely in bed.

Grass Pollen: microscopic grains of pollen are released into the atmosphere in the summer months and cause many problems for allergy sufferers.

Animal danders: this means the scurf, fluff, hair and scale shed from pets. The most allergy-provoking of these are dog, cat and horse danders.

These materials (called allergens) can worsen atopic eczema, or just keep it simmering, by two mechanisms:

(a) By coming into direct contact with pre-existing inflamed skin and causing an increase in the itch. It is almost exactly the same reaction as occurs in the whites of the eyes with hay fever – the tissue becomes swollen and itchy, and weeps.

(b) By 'overloading' the body's defence mechanisms against all the substances causing allergy. In other words, if the body is constantly producing allergic reactions then there is a high level of chemicals produced by these reactions circulating in the blood, and they keep the skin constantly under inflammation from within.

To summarize: atopic eczema is an allergic inflammation of the skin. Substances which provoke this are thought to be foods or inhaled allergy material such as pollen and dust mites. To tackle the root of the problem we must deal with the substances which produce the allergic reaction.

The management of atopic eczema now depends on whether it is of the mild, moderate or severe variety.

Mild eczema is only slight, with occasional redness and itch of the skin.
Moderate is persistent, involving patchy areas which do not resolve with simple measures.
Severe eczema is chronic and involves widespread areas. There is constant scratching, the skin is raw and weeping and sleep and social activities are disrupted.

Whether the eczema is mild, moderate or severe, I believe that attention to the underlying allergic cause is important – otherwise you will end up treating continually without ever getting to the kernel of the problem. Having said that, for most mild cases only occasional treatment is needed and in these children it is of dubious value to become too aggressive in an allergic approach – the benefits may not justify the effort.

Management

Bear in mind that atopic eczema implies an allergic inflammation of the skin, and so both must be dealt with – the inflamed skin must be healed and the allergic causes dealt with.

- In *mild eczema*, as we discussed in Chapter 1, inflamed skin can be healed with the use of cortisone creams or ointments. For many cases of mild eczema this is all the treatment that is necessary, the occasional and correct application of a mild cortisone-based cream such as 1% hydrocortisone two or three times daily during flare ups will suffice. (See appendix 1 for further details about cortisone creams.) More often than not the sensible use of these creams will give great relief, allow the skin to heal, and do away with the need for a more heavy-handed, time consuming approach.

  However, if the eczema, while still mild, needs constant applications of creams or ointments (no matter how low strength and safe these are) then perhaps a close look at allergic causes is justified. This is discussed in the next section.

- In *moderate eczema* the skin inflammation is persistent, does not settle with simple measures or low strength cortisone cream or ointments and is causing disruption of sleep and social activities. An easy way out of this problem is to use much higher strength cortisone creams on a regular basis. However, there are problems associated with this approach and so a look at the allergic basis now becomes important.

  Substances which cause an allergic reaction are known as *allergens*. Atopic eczema may be caused by something in the child's diet, or by an irritant in the air which the child breathes in. The inhaled substances may cause skin reactions by settling directly onto the already inflamed skin.

  Which of these various reactions is important in your child depends to a great extent on age and how widespread the eczema is. In general terms children up to two years of age are more bothered by foodstuffs than air-borne allergens such as house dust mites, pollens or animal danders. After two years of age these two types of allergy substances may work together to keep the eczema 'ticking over'. After five years of age the air-borne allergens are likely to be the most important culprits.

Treatment plan for persisting mild to moderate atopic eczema:
For a child up to two years old you should eliminate the following from the diet:

- all dairy products (milk, cream, yoghurt, butter, cheese, ice-cream);
- eggs in any form (scrambled, poached, quiches, and so on);
- chocolate and foods which contain chocolate;
- unnecessary artificial colourings and preservatives in all foodstuffs, but especially those listed in Appendix 4.

23

Continue to use the cortisone-based creams prescribed by your doctor and use them as he has suggested (and not as your next-door neighbour feels you should!).

If your child has symptoms suggesting inhaled allergy problems such as conjunctivitis (red, itchy, watery eyes) rhinitis (blocked, stuffy, sneezy nose) or asthma (coughs and wheezes) then a separate aggressive anti-allergy approach should also be considered. This is discussed when we consider *severe* eczema.

Using these guidelines for a minimum of six weeks, you should notice some improvement in your child's skin, with the need for less use of creams or ointments. If this approach works then let your doctor know so that he is aware of the connection between the eczema and any allergy, but, more importantly, so that he can advise you on the diet your child is taking to ensure it is not inadequate. For example, a dairy-produce-free diet in a small, growing child may leave him deficient in calcium and vitamins. These may need to be replaced (although they are supplemented in many of the alternative soya-based feeds for children.)

With any luck the eczema will become much more manageable so that your child's skin recovers well and looks much healthier. In time he/she may lose the tendency to eczema altogether, or at least be only occasionally troubled by a mild form, which should settle quickly with the correct use of cream or ointment.

For children over two years of age both foods and air-borne allergens, especially house dust mites, are important. In particular, if your child shows other features of allergy such as conjunctivitis (red, itchy, watery eyes) rhinitis (blocked, stuffy, sneezy nose) or asthma (coughs and wheezes) then the air-borne allergens almost certainly have a role to play in the eczema as well.

In this situation the dietary plan set out for children under two should be implemented, *combined* with a vigorous anti-house dust mite programme. The anti-dust mite programme is set out on page 28. In addition all furry or hairy pets should be banned from the house and all traces of their hair/fur/dander hoovered and damp dusted away from every room. This plan will cut down dramatically on the amount of materials which provoke the allergy in the child's environment.

Please continue to use the cortisone creams as prescribed by your doctor as he has suggested.

This programme should continue for six weeks and should produce a much improved skin with a decreased need for creams. As time progresses the eczema may clear altogether or at least become only occasionally troublesome and should settle quickly on these occasions with the correct application of a cream. At the end of the six week trial consult with your doctor or local dietitian on how to phase in reduced quantities of the foods you have been cutting out, but don't allow chocolate and unnecessary food additives until the skin has been totally clear for six months.

In addition to the creams and anti-allergy programme it is important to remember that some things will irritate sensitive skin at the best of times and so should be avoided in children with eczema. These include washing powders and certain clothing materials. At the end of the next section I have set out guidelines on these but a more detailed discussion of washing powders appears on page 78 and suitable clothing is dealt with in Appendix 5.

A management routine for severe eczema

In severe eczema your child has chronic dry, red, sensitive, itchy skin that looks rough and unhealthy. Nights on end are spent scratching and the bed linen is often a mess of blood and scale. This type of eczema is extremely distressing and can disturb your whole life – parents often take it in turn to sleep with the affected child to try and prevent the constant scratching. Life revolves around distracting the scratching fingers. The child almost certainly has multiple allergy problems such as conjunctivitis, rhinitis and asthma, and may be well below average height and weight.

In this situation everything that can be done should be done to relieve the misery of the family and child. No doctor worth his salt, who really cares for the children he treats, can argue with a more aggressive plan of management if it is patently obvious that his own ideas on treatment are not working.

The following plan is based on the simple belief that atopic eczema is fundamentally an allergic skin condition. Consequently, any programme that reduces the amount of material which provokes allergy in the child's environment should, in turn, reduce the child's eczema.

I have set out this plan in four stages but they all should be put into effect at the same time. In essence your child's skin is healed using a special cortisone cream regime and, as the creams are being phased out, the aggressive anti-allergy programme should come into effect so that the eczema does not erupt again.

Stage 1. The first step is to heal your child's inflamed skin. A 'step-ladder' approach to clearing the eczema is given in Appendix 1. The idea is that you obtain from your doctor a selection of cortisone-based creams, ranging from very strong to very weak. Apply the strongest of these creams to all areas where there is eczema (except the face, where a different approach is used) and rub it in well. Continue this twice daily *for as long as it takes* to produce a total clearance of the eczema with resulting healthy-looking skin. Then apply the next strength down twice daily (*even though the skin is clear*) for about five to ten days (this will depend on how severe the original eczema was). Then use the next strength down and so on until the skin is 'weaned off' the need for strong creams and is maintained healthy on only the weak variety. As the lower-strength creams are being introduced the eczema may occasionally break through –if this happens then go back to the next strength up for a few extra days and attempt to come down again. With time these outbreaks will become less and less likely.

For the face a similar approach can be used except that only one step above hydrocortisone 1% (see Appendix 1) is used to induce the initial clearance and the time taken to 'come down the ladder' is longer.

If you use this plan *do not skip the various stages* when weaning down otherwise the skin will not heal properly and a rebound eczema will occur at lower strengths.

Stage 2. Now we come to the anti-allergy programme. I have already explained how foods or substances in the air can cause or exacerbate eczema. We have to deal with these materials as follows:

If the problem is caused by *consumed allergens* we attempt to identify and remove those foodstuffs likely to be causing internal allergy. No allergy test will pin-point all these problem foods accurately so your child must be put through an 'elimination and challenge' routine. This means that the foods most likely to provoke an allergic reaction are removed for four weeks minimum and then gradually reintroduced. As each food is reintroduced any signs of deterioration in skin control are noted and that food then classed as 'unsafe' and kept out of the child's diet completely for at least six months.

In the list below, those foods on the left are avoided during the first four weeks and those on the right are allowed.

Avoid	*Allowed*
milk	beef
cheese	lamb
yoghurt	rye crispbreads
chocolate	tea
butter	coffee
ice-cream	soya

margarine	vegetables (except those
all sweets, crisps	listed on the left)
and nuts	Granose margarine
eggs	rice
fish	pears
chicken	bananas
pork or bacon	rhubarb
all citrus fruits	potatoes
tomatoes	ginger
peas	
sprouts	
sweetcorn	
wheat from any source,	
bread, biscuits, cake, etc.	
any food with artificial	
colourings or preservatives.	

This regime should be continued for a minimum of three weeks and must not be broken. If your child improves, then the chances are that the eczema is aggravated by a strong food allergy. Individual foods should now be reintroduced at the rate of one per week and any deterioration noted. Those foods positively shown to cause a worsening of the eczema are then avoided totally. Interestingly, after about six months on a diet free of the provocative foods, they can often be tolerated in small amounts. Those foods which should – if at all possible – be kept away always from the child as they are real trouble-makers in eczema are chocolates, coloured sweets and drinks and processed foods with the notorious 'E' numbers as set out in Appendix 4.

Incidentally, it is worth noting that certain foods, especialy citrus fruits and tomatoes, irritate sensitive skin when *handled*. Avoid this if at all possible.

If you embark upon this approach please insist that a dietitian is involved so that your child is not left deficient in important minerals and vitamins. Remember – we are trying to solve a problem, not replace it with another!

If the problem is caused by *air-borne allergens* and you have furry or hairy pets, then *out they go* from the living areas of the house. There should be *no* compromise on this. The hair, fur and dander that these animals may have shed throughout the house will now need to be hoovered and damp dusted away, and the measures against dust mites (given below) will also eradicate animal dander. *Do not allow these pets back in the house again!*

Next you must work on one of the most important causes of chronic eczema in children, the house dust mite. This is a tiny insect that lives in and feeds off ordinary household dust and contributes to symptoms affecting eyes nose, chest and skin. In children with severe eczema then the following (fairly dramatic) regime should be completed. It aims to reduce to zero the amount of house dust in the child's environment, especially at home. Before embarking upon this routine have your child allergy tested (as described in my book *How to Cope with Your Child's Allergies*), to ensure that there is a positive reaction to dust mites.

How to get rid of house dust mites

- Use *synthetic* (or *cotton*) *pillows and bedlinen*. Use polyester or similar man-made fillings for pillows. Wash the duvet every two or three weeks and the sheets and pillow cases each week. If your child prefers blankets to a duvet choose acrilan or cotton ones because these are easier to wash and dry than the woollen types. Both the synthetic and cotton fibres are good 'low-allergy' materials and dust mites don't thrive in them.
- The mattress and pillows should be enclosed inside *plastic covers*. Allow a little air into each with a gap somewhere in the covering. Air any pillows or mattress enclosed like this at least once a month. A good source of suitable plastic covers is Keys of Clacton Ltd., 132 Old Road, Clacton-on-Sea, Essex CO15, 3AJ, which operates a mail-order service.
- Take the mattress out into the sun as often as possible and let the air get at it.
- *Vacuum-clean* the room including the carpets, curtains upholstery and even the mattresses and blankets. Don't forget under the bed!
- All clothes and shoes should be put away in *wardrobes*. Dressing-gowns should not hang behind doors.
- Use *light-weight curtains* or, better still use *blinds* instead.
- Use a *damp duster* rather than a dry one, which tends to redistribute the dust.
- Use a spray called Tymasil (available from your chemist or doctor) to kill off the dust-mite population in the mattress.
- In the rest of the house use *linoleum* or *wood flooring* rather than rugs and carpet. Cut down on the use of woolly rugs, velvet curtains, and the like.
- Vacuum as often as possible but empty the bag more frequently than usual and damp-dust skirting boards, mantlepieces and sills.
- The entire house must be sprayed with *Acclaim* (*methoprene*) which kills the mites. This is available from major chemists and is also

obtainable as IGRS from Sweetwell Ltd., 2 Mount Place, Lewes, Sussex by mail order. Spraying needs to be repeated indefinitely once a month. The agent is non-toxic and has been passed by the World Health Organization as safe. It may take about three months for these manoeuvres to work because of the time to get the house ultra-clean.

- Paint the walls of your child's bedroom with Artilin-3A. This is an ordinary-looking household paint (available in satin-matt emulsion and gloss finish) specially formulated to kill house dust mites on contact. Its success lies essentially in the control of larvae. Artilin-3A stops the development of eggs laid by dust mites. Not only is the mite killed on contact with any painted surface, but eggs laid on it will not hatch. In addition Artilin-3A destroys the microscopic organisms on which the mite feeds and will remain active for between three to five years. In Britain this paint can be ordered from Gem Services (UK) Ltd., Harwal Works, Elliot Street, Silsden, Keighley, West Yorkshire BD20 0DP (tel: Steeton (0535) 56010). In Ireland from: DJB Imports Ltd, P.O. Box 22, Dun Laoire, Co. Dublin (tel: (01) 809133).

Stage 3. The next step is to identify and treat any other allergy problems that your child might be suffering from – these tend to be allergies of the eyes, nose and chest. Do bear in mind that your anti-allergy programme in stage 2 will pay dividends soon so that the eye, nose and chest symptons will also reduce. However, in the meantime, give your child a break from these associated irritating conditions.

If the eyes are affected an anti-allergy preparation called sodium cromoglycate (trade name Opticrom) is applied four times daily (two drops) to give relief. These drops are *totally safe*, and can be used indefinitely or until the stage 2 anti-allergy programme becomes effective.

In many children with severe eczema a condition called allergic rhinitis is also present. This is an allergic swelling of the inside lining of the nose leading to problems such as blockage, itch, mucus drip and sneezing. A drug called Beclomethasone is used to help this. It comes in two forms – drops called Betnesol and a spray called Beconase. If the nose is very blocked then the drops are used initially to clear the blockage and allow the spray to maintain the improvement. If the nose is not first unblocked, the spray will be totally ineffective.

To clear a very blocked nose the following routine is adopted. Your child gets into one or other of the two positions as shown in the diagram. While in this position two drops are instilled into each nostril

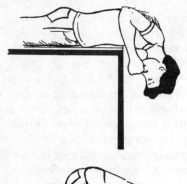

Choose either of these two positions

and your child stays like this for a minimum of three minutes. This routine is performed twice daily until the nose is cleared – this may take anything from a few days to a few months. When the nose has been restored as close to normal as possible then the spray form (Beconase) is used to maintain the improvement.

The medicine in the drops and spray, Beclomethasone, is a form of cortisone. It is completely safe and not absorbed into the blood stream and will not cause any damage to the nose in the long or short term. The reason behind this routine is twofold – it restores the lining of the nose to normal (which removes one of the many irritating problems these children have to deal with) and it blocks the absorption of other allergens which might gain entry to the body via the nose.

If your child has asthma an assortment of medicines can be used here. The full details of these can be obtained in my book *Coping Successfully with Your Child's Asthma*, published by Sheldon Press.

This is a very aggressive approach and one that is extremely time consuming. However, if you have a child with severe eczema you will know only too well how dreadful the condition is and how desperate all concerned will be to improve the child's lot in life. Desperate problems sometimes demand equally dramatic remedies and I am quite sure the programme will produce good results.

To summarize:

(a) Skin control is important. A step-ladder approach, with different-strength creams will tackle the skin inflammations.

(b) An aggressive anti-allergy programme will reduce the child's exposure to those foods, dust mites and animal danders which keep the eczema simmering away. In addition, by keeping dust mites and animal danders to the bare minimum, associated allergies (such as rhinitis, conjunctivitis, and asthma) should be relieved.

There are two other methods which doctors occasionally use when dealing with atopic eczema.

● Your child may be given Nalcrom (sodium cromoglycate). This is an anti-allergy medicine which is swallowed 30 minutes before meals and blocks the effects of food induced allergic reactions. It is very safe, but not always effective even where a definite food allergy component exists in the eczema. Certainly there is no substitute for the correct identification and removal of the offending foods involved in eczema. Nalcrom tends to be used in children, in conjunction with the previous plan, where there are multiple allergy problems and the diet is becoming too-restrictive.

● It is also possible to desensitize the child against the main substance he/she is allergic to – especially grass pollens and house dust mites. Desensitization means that a series of injections (containing extracts of what the child is allergic to) is given to stimulate immunity and dampen down the allergic reaction. The injections are continued on a monthly basis for between one and three years depending on severity of symptoms and response to the therapy. This programme must only be carried out in properly equipped centres where the doctors involved know what they are doing and can deal with any side effects. If you cannot satisfy yourself that these conditions are met then do not subject your child to this treatment.

Finally, some important extra points to be aware of so that your child has the best chance of beating this problem.

● *No furry pets* should ever be allowed in the house. If you have one – get rid of it and vacuum carefully all areas where the pet has been. The dander from furry pets is very allergy-provoking and adds to the total 'allergy load' your child has to deal with.

● Some *fabrics* irritate sensitive skin, especially wool and nylon. Make sure that pure cotton is always next to your child's skin and don't overdress your child.

- Use only *mild detergents* for washing your child's clothes and avoid the strong biological enzyme powders. Rinse all clothes very carefully.
- Use simple *non-scented soaps* for washing.

Complications

Children with eczema are prone to getting bacterial and fungal infections of their skin. This can be minimized by aiming for optimum skin control and ensuring an early treatment of any infection.

Two other problems that occur in connection with eczema are **warts** and **molluscum contagiosum**. These are viral infections and are like first cousins to one another. The viruses produce swellings of the skin surface that look unsightly and spread quickly. They are dealt with very effectively using *cryosurgery* (see Appendix 3).

As many as 90% of children with eczema have other allergy problems affecting eyes, nose, chest etc., and full details on how to deal with these are available in my books *How To Cope With Your Child's Allergies* and *Coping Successfully With Your Child's Asthma*.

Children with eczema occasionally get bad attacks of *cold sores*, a virus infection of the lips and face (see **herpes simplex**). The virus is a real nuisance as it stubbornly clings to the affected tissue and reactivates every now and then. Sometimes a cold wind on the face or even strong sunlight is enough to start a fresh outbreak of cold sores. When this occurs tiny blisters form in the affected area with occasional ulcers in the mouth. It is very painful and unsightly.

However, children with eczema can develop a much more widespread form of cold sores, where large areas of the skin are affected and the virus enters the bloodstream to attack internal organs. This is a very, very serious, life-threatening complication. It is called *eczema herpeticum* and, though rare, should be dealt with very quickly. If your child has cold sores and the blisters appear to be spreading beyond the usual site then have your doctor check the situation as soon as possible. There is an excellent drug called *Zovirax* (acyclovir) which is used in the hospital treatment of eczema herpeticum and it gives excellent results.

All routine immunizations can be given to children with eczema except the vaccination against smallpox. Never allow your child to be given this type of vaccination and never allow anyone with a recent smallpox vaccination within close range of your child. This is because the smallpox vaccine can produce a very dangerous reaction called *vaccinia*.

Atopic dermatitis. See *Atopic Eczema.*

Birth marks

These are a form of persistent skin swelling or discoloration, present when the child is born. The following are the most common and their management is described:

- *'Stork mark'.* A pinkish bruise-like mark found on the upper eyelids and nape of the neck. The name recalls the mythical stork who brought the child to the mother and suggests these were the areas that the child was held in-transit in the stork's beak. These areas should be left alone as the discolouration fades in time; marks on the back of the neck may persist for years but are usually hidden by hair.
- *'Port-wine stain'.* This is a purplish-blue discolouration of the skin which often covers large areas of the face and neck and limbs. A port-wine stain on one side of the face only, particularly if it involves the forehead, may be associated with a problem inside the brain on the same side. The brain problem can cause convulsions and mental retardation and for this reason such children are usually carefully screened for signs of this complication.

  Unfortunately the port-wine stain birth mark is extremely resistant to treatment and most therapies are aimed at disguising it with make-up. Some smaller areas can be removed surgically and the area grafted with clear skin from another part of the body.
- *Strawberry haemangiomata.* See **haemangiomata.**
- *Moles.* See **moles.**
- *Mongolian blue spot.* This is really a racial characteristic and of no real significance apart from its cosmetic effect. It consists of dark blue areas of skin on the lower back and buttocks – occasionally it involves the entire back with patches on limbs. It is found on black, Asian and Eskimo babies. It usually fades during the first year of life. The *mongolian* tag does not imply any relationship to Down's syndrome.

Blepharitis

This is an inflammation of the skin of the outer edges of the eyelids. There are two types: in one there is scaling and irritability of the eyelid edges only, and in the other an infection sets into the eyelash hair follicles. The first type is often associated with dandruff and shows as white scaling at the roots of the eyelashes. The second type usually shows with small infected areas with soreness and redness of the eyelids. Both are treated similarly by, first, dealing with any underlying causes such as *dandruff*; second, soaking away any crusts of infection or scale with cotton wool and warm water; and finally, applying an antibiotic ointment at night to kill off the infection.

Boils

Boils are an infection which develops at the root of a hair follicle. They are also called *furuncles*. The boil starts as a tender red lump which gets bigger and more painful until it comes to a head and the pus escapes. This may take up to five days to occur. Boils often occur in clusters.

In general, such infections are trivial and do not require antibiotic tablets or creams – nature will produce a quicker and better cure by allowing the boil to develop and discharge. You can help nature by following these guidelines:

- Clean the surrounding skin with an antiseptic or surgical spirit.
- Put a piece of clean dressing over the boil to reduce contact irritation.
- Do not squeeze the boil.
- Take your child to a doctor if there are signs of red streaks stretching from the boil along the skin and some glands start to swell.

If your child has recurring boils then have his/her urine tested for possible diabetes – if this is clear then some doctors treat the inside of the nose with a special antibiotic cream as the 'bug' which causes the boils often lies in this area and is passed on the finger tips after rubbing the nose.

Bruises

A bruise occurs when blood vessels under the skin are damaged and blood leaks into surrounding tissue. The area looks red initially, then bluish-black. As nature sets about healing the area and absorbing the leaking blood, further colour changes occur. The bruise turns yellow, brown and finally disappears. Some bruises can take weeks to clear.

Remember that small children have soft skin and tissue that will bruise easily compared to that of adults. In addition, the games children play tend to result in frequent bruises and multiple battle scars.

There is no magic treatment for bruising. All you can really do is apply a cold compress against the affected area.

If your child has a very large bruise – say, twice the size of an adult hand, then have your doctor check that no major accidents have occurred.

The only other significant point to look for with bruises is if a lot seem to occur together and don't clear within a reasonable length of time. If this occurs, check with your family doctor.

Burns

Burns and scalds affect not only the immediate surface layer of the skin but also the important blood vessels underneath. Heat penetrates the skin, causing it to rupture and *plasma*, the colourless part of the blood, to be released. In small burns the plasma forms a blister on the surface of the skin whereas in larger burns, where the skin surface peels away, it seeps from the raw area. If a sufficiently large area is burned or scalded then large amounts of plasma are lost from the body. In small children this can seriously reduce their total blood volume and cause quite dramatic problems. For this reason, the area of skin involved in burns and scalds is more important than the depth.

Burns and scalds are extremely painful and cause great distress to children. Even relatively small burns are troublesome. (Indeed the pain element is a good sign as it shows that the nerve endings are intact. In severe, deep burns the nerve endings may be destroyed and so the area is relatively painless. However the lack of pain is not a good sign, reflecting as it does, the depth of tissue destruction.)

Naked flames and scalding

Similar treatments are used for burns due to naked flames and scalds. First, remove the child from the source of heat – douse the flames or roll the child in a blanket or carpet to smother any flames from burning clothes. Then cool the burned area as soon as possible by immersing in cold water or holding under the running cold tap. If clothes are soaked in boiling water, plunge the child or affected limb into the bath and hose the area with the shower head while waiting for the bath to fill. If no shower head is available then roll the child around in the filling bath. Continue to cool the affected area by immersion or under cold water for at least five minutes. This will help with the immediate pain of the burn and also reduce the amount of damage done to the blood vessels. It may also help reduce the loss of plasma.

An exception to the above guidelines is when the burns are due to immersion in *boiling oil*, strong *acids*, or *alkalis* – here the sooner the clothes are removed the better and you can justifiably tear at the child's garments for as quick a removal as possible.

If the burned area needs medical attention, wrap the child's affected limbs or entire body in a clean sheet and take him to the nearest hospital. Decisions should be made here as to the competence and facilities of your family doctor in dealing with such emergencies. In an ideal world he should be able to provide first-aid treatment, assess the burn and make arrangements for hospital treatment if this is considered appropriate. However, some surgeries are not up to this and so, rather than delay good help by going to inadequate facilities, short-circuit the system and go straight to the casualty department of the nearest hospital.

As a guide the following rules apply:

- Burns affecting up to 1 square inch (6 sq. cm) of skin should at least be seen by your family doctor.
- Burns of the size of your own hand are much more important and should be dealt with fairly quickly – either by your GP if he is up to it or by the casualty department of hospital.
- Burns greater than the size of an adult hand should be dealt with in hospital.
- Burns over *joints* such as the elbow, wrist or knee should be seen by hospital doctors. This is to prevent a type of healing (called contractures) forming which might interfere with the mobility of the joint.

For burns small enough to treat at home the following rules apply:

- *Don't interfere* with any *blisters* as they act as a barrier against infection.
- *Don't use ointments* or *grease* on the damaged skin.
- Apply only a *sterile adhesive dressing* or *clean lint* to the affected area.

Electrical burns

Immediately remove the child from the source of the burn, taking care not to handle any live wires yourself! Use a wooden broom handle to push away any exposed wires. Electrical burns may seem trivial as quite often the only visible sign of damage is a blackened pinpoint area. However, the current tends to 'fan out' under the skin and there may well be a large wedge of burned tissue underneath the normal-looking skin. There is little you can do in practical terms for such burns and as a general rule they should all be checked by (at least) your family doctor.

Sunburn

Sunburn will range from lobster-red areas of skin (which feel very tender and hot to the touch) to severe sunstroke with shivering, nausea and vomiting. The sunburnt skin may blister.

In general, these burns are unlikely to ever cause major medical problems but can leave a child quite unwell for days. If the area involved is only sunburned (red, hot to touch and feeling tight) then a liberal coating of a simple moisturizer such as Nivea cream is sufficient. Apply the cream every three or four hours and keep the child in a cool, darkened room. Encourage the intake of fluids. If a larger area is involved and the child is distressed then have your doctor assess the situation. He may well prescribe a mild hydrocortisone cream (see Appendix 1) so as to reduce the inflammation of the skin and promote a quicker resolution of the problem.

Sunstroke usually looks more dramatic than it actually is medically. The child should be kept cool and given plenty of fluids to sip on. He/she should be nursed under a clean single sheet and the sunburned areas covered liberally with a moisturizer such as Nivea cream. If your child is shivering a lot and seems unduly distressed then have your family doctor check the situation.

With a view to prevention of sunburn, do use your common sense. Children have very soft, sensitive skin and cannot tolerate excessive exposure to sun, especially in the British Isles where sunny days are not terribly frequent! It is tempting to make full use of every minute of sunshine and lie out in the open for hours. Red-haired children are most at risk from sunburn, followed by blonds, brunettes and then those with dark hair. Use an appropriate sunblock and remember that small children may run around totally naked on a sunny day and get burnt on places you wouldn't usually expect! Rub sunblock creams on buttocks especially in this situation. Your chemist can advise on an appropriate sunblock cream. Remember also that;

- sun is reflected off water, so take care if out in boats;
- veiled sun can still burn;
- wind can cool and mislead as to the extent of sunburn occurring;
- children will be the last to recognize they are burning – so keep a close eye on them in sunshine.

Candida

This is also kown as *monilia*, *thrush* or *yeast*. It is a fungus-type 'bug' which just loves certain types of skin, especially inflamed skin such as occurs in *eczema*. The 'bug' itself is a normal, *healthy*, inhabitant of the body and only becomes a nuisance if it congregates in one area of tissue and looks as if it's settling in forever.

37

In babies the usual areas of candida infection are the mouth and nappy areas. The most likely way in which candida becomes established in the mouth is via inadequately sterilized bottles and teats. It produces white, cheesy patches inside the mouth – especially on the cheeks, palate and tongue. The patches sometimes look like curdled milk but if you try and wipe them away they either stick or come off, leaving raw areas underneath. The mouth is usually sore and, for this reason, the child may go off feeds even though hungry.

Candida also likes to settle on damaged or inflamed skin and the two next most frequent areas of infection are the nappy area and skin which is affected by *eczema*. The nappy area is most vulnerable because of the problem of nappy rash (see *napkin dermatitis*). In nappy rash, red and inflamed skin is kept covered with an often wet cloth napkin and encased further in plastic pants. This produces an ideal environment for candida to grow and the 'bug' will settle on the skin and multiply very quickly. This will produce an even more irritating rash (and more irritable baby). Clues which suggest that candida is becoming established in nappy area are the presence of a rash in the folds of the skin of the groin; and red pinpoint spots form around the rash and seem to be spreading well away from the original area.

A child with *atopic eczema* will have inflamed skin which candida loves to feed off. Quite often the candida infection on top of the eczema may be the reason for the skin appearing to heal poorly despite adequate treatment. In this situation the candida must be effectively dealt with before any other treatment is tried. Clues which suggest candida is settling on the eczema are an unexpected increase in itching and pinpoint red areas around the eczematous skin.

Candida is treated either locally or generally. In a local treatment, an anti-candida paint or cream is applied directly to the affected area, two or three times daily, until the infection clears. Local treatments include a purple paint called *gentian violet*. This is a rather old-fashioned remedy and leads to staining of clothes and skin for days. It is effective and cheap and for these reasons still widely used. Other local treatments include creams and mouthwashes too numerous to mention here but set out in Appendix 2. Quite often the anti-candida medicine is combined with a mild hydrocortisone medicine to produce a preparation which promotes quicker healing.

For recurring or persisting candida infection a general approach is used. This means that anti-candida medicines are swallowed three or four times daily for about a week to eradicate all forms of candida, especially any persisting reservoirs in the intestines. This is particularly important for candida nappy rashes which seem particularly resistant to treatment. In such situations the bowel actions may contain lots of the candida bug which can easily attack the skin of the napkin area. Where this is considered a possibility then an aggressive anti-candida regime usually brings quick results.

Cellulitis

This is a painful, red and tender swelling of soft tissue – usually of the limbs. The underlying cause is a bacterial infection, although often the exact area where the bugs have penetrated the skin is impossible to detect. The infection will commonly start with a small pinpoint area of redness that looks as if it might come to a head. Instead the infection spreads underneath the skin surface producing pain and swelling. The area feels hot to the touch. If left unchecked a red line will be seen to extend from the original area up to the nearest glands. These in turn will swell and become very tender. Your child will be unwilling to move the limb and may feel unwell, with fever and shivering. If you observe these symptoms take your child to the doctor immediately.

The commonest 'bug' which causes this problem is called *streptococcus*, which also is involved in most bacterial infections of the throat. The treatment is simple but very important. The affected limb is rested, raised in the air and high doses of antibiotics are taken.

Chicken-pox

This is a common viral illness which is very infectious in children. In younger children the symptoms tend to be mild and often of little consequence whereas in older children a more unpleasant few days can be anticipated.

The incubation period of the virus is 17–21 days. This means that the actual symptoms may not develop for up to 21 days (but usually around 17 days) after exposure to someone else who has the same infection. The first signs are red pimples on the skin (anywhere, but usually on the trunk) which develop into blisters. These are very itchy and fragile – easily rubbed off, leaving raw areas which heal with a scab. The full-blown condition may take up to five days to become fully established and during this time new pimples and blisters appear just as the earlier ones are heading towards the healing stage.

In its most severe form a very extensive rash covers the child from head to toe, including scalp, inside the mouth and ears, genitalia and anus. The intense itch leads to a lot of scratching and an increase in the general irritability of the child, who will be feverish and generally

39

unwell. It is a good idea to keep the scabs under observation to ensure that no infection is settling in on top of the raw area. In general, anything that can make your child's condition more tolerable should be offered – especially lots of love and plenty of hugs. Sponge the child down if the fever is high and encourage him/her to take plenty of fluids. The itching can be helped by frequent lukewarm baths in which a cupful of sodium bicarbonate has been dissolved. In between the baths dab some calamine lotion onto the spots and, if necessary, ask your doctor for a mild *antihistamine* for use at night. This will reduce the itch somewhat and may also partially sedate, thus allowing for an easier night all round! For small babies, leave without nappies as long as possible, and – this applies to all age groups – keep the fingernails as short and clean as possible.

Chilblains

These are painful red swellings which occur on the fingers and toes (usually) in cold weather. They are a response of very small blood vessels to cold and extremely difficult to manage. The mainstay of treatment is to ensure the toes and fingers are kept warm and protected during cold spells – cotton socks and mittens under wool often provide best results. Some liniment and ointment which reduce itching and cause a localized increase in blood supply are occasionally helpful. The most effective of these contain *camphor* and your chemist will guide you on selecting one if needed.

Cold sores See *herpes simplex*.

Contact eczema

This is also called *contact dermatitis*. It occurs when your child's skin has become inflamed by contact with an irritating substance. If you look back at Chapter 1, where I described the changes occurring with inflammation, you will see that the normal, healthy protective outer layer of skin becomes disrupted, leading to redness, itch and weeping. The inflammation can be due to an allergic reaction or simply an irritating reaction; for example, if egg white falls directly onto some children's skin it will cause an immediate eczema – this is an *allergic mechanism*. However, urine-soaked nappies can also cause a localized eczema simply by being too close to skin for too long – this is an *irritant mechanism*.

It is unusual for children to have a long-standing contact eczema as few will ever be too close to most irritating substances for very long. The most common type of contact eczema in children is nappy rash (see *napkin dermatitis*).

If you have a child with contact eczema try and help your doctor in his detective work of tracking down the offending substances. Find out:

- when the rash started;
- what makes it worse;
- how many episodes there have been previously;
- whether it varies from season to season;
- in what type of environment it seems to occur;
- which areas it affects;
- what types of plants and chemicals the child is likely to encounter.

The commonest causes of irritant eczema are detergents, perfumed soaps and shampoos, cheap jewellery, some cosmetics (particularly those which contain lanolin), some shoes which have troublesome chemicals in their material, plants (especially compositae, primulae, chrysanthemums), foods, wool, alcohol, and preservatives in medical creams. The treatments usually involve the use of a mild cortisone cream (see Appendix 1) to reduce the inflammation, followed by regular moisturizer which acts as a lubricant and barrier. Any co-existing infection will need to be dealt with, as will the removal of the underlying cause.

For persisting or recurring cases a testing procedure called *patch testing* is carried out. This involves placing a number of different substances onto the skin (usually the back) and leaving them attached to the area for 48 hours. After this time the area is examined for signs of eczema against the individual substances and a record made of which caused skin inflammation. Sensible decisions can then be made so that contact with such inflammation-causing material is avoided.

Cradle cap

This is a thick brown layer of *crust* on the scalp of young babies which is difficult to remove. It is occasionally due to inadequate washing of the scalp because an inexperienced mother may be hesistant in applying much pressure near the new baby's 'soft' spots on the head. The crusting eventually peels away leaving normal, healthy scalp but this can be speeded up by applying softening agents directly onto the scale. Olive-oil – warmed slightly – is massaged onto the crust and left for 30 minutes. It can then be gently washed off with a mild baby shampoo. Some of the scale will separate with each application to the point where eventually the scalp is free from all scale. Another trick is to wash the scalp with a solution of sodium bicarbonate (one teaspoon to a pint – or half a litre – of water). In resistant cases a coal-tar solution can be applied as an ointment at night and as a shampoo in the morning. Do remember that, while the crusting may look unpleasant, it will do no harm to the child or his/her scalp. Indeed if left alone the scale would eventually separate out itself.

Dandruff

This is a small scale formation on the scalp leading to flaking onto the shoulders and forehead. As the scale falls over the forehead it sticks to the eyebrows and eyelashes leading to a localized irritation at these points. In some severe forms the scale forms a thick stubborn layer on the scalp which must be removed before any other treatments will work.

There are many proprietary brands of anti-dandruff shampoo but the most effective contains *selenium sulphide* and is marketed as *Selsun*. This can be used two or three times a week for clearance and then weekly to maintain control.

Remember that if there is a stubborn thick scale no medication will work – the scale acts as a barrier and must be removed. This can be achieved by soaking the scale in warm olive oil and leaving for 30 minutes before shampooing out. There has been recent evidence to suggest that some forms of dandruff are caused by a *candida* infection of the scalp. If your child has a very resistant form of dandruff it might be worth asking your doctor about this connection. An anti-candida shampoo containing *ketoconazole* (Nizoral is the trade name) is very effective in some dandruff conditions but may need to be used for up to 12 weeks.

Dermatitis See *atopic eczema*; *contact eczema*.

Dermatophytosis Another name for *ringworm*.

Drug eruptions.

These are skin problems which children may develop in response to having taken medication – whether prescribed or bought over the counter. The simplest case would be where the skin erupts in a rash in an otherwise healthy child after beginning medication. The eruption usually disappears in ten days once the treatment is stopped, but will reappear if the treatment is ever prescribed again. There are many types of drug eruption, ranging from spots, itchy wheals, bruising, red blisters, redness and itching to a severe skin shedding with vomiting.

Suspect a drug reaction in any generalized symmetrical skin outbreak that appears suddenly – especially if your child has recently started to take some form of medication. Skin reactions generally occur within one week, although penicillin (if injected into a muscle) may not show up for over ten days after the beginning of treatment. Do remember that many simple cough bottles and decongestants contain different types of medicine, all of which have the potential to produce skin eruptions in sensitive children.

Stopping the medicine is all that is required in most cases to clear the skin eruption – occasionally some mild cortisone-based creams are used to promote a quicker healing process.

If you suspect a medicine has caused a skin reaction in your child, it is *very important* to tell your doctor so that he can confirm your suspicions and make a note in his medical records. You might also get your child to wear a MedicAlert bracelet with this information printed inside it. This will prevent him/her accidentally being given a dose of the offending drug.

Ecchymosis See *bruises*.

Eczema See *atopic eczema*; *contact eczema*.

Erysipelas

This is a superficial form of skin infection like *cellulitis*, with a rapidly spreading redness, swelling and pain in the affected area. It is due to a specific bacterium called *streptococcus* and can occur on the face, limbs and tummy of children. The infection is of the superficial skin layers and classically affects the face, beginning on the cheeks and spreading to form a 'butterfly' shape in a few days. If erysipelas reaches this stage the child is usually unwell with a high fever, chills, nausea and headaches.

The treatment involves *penicillin*, given in the form of tablets or injection, depending on how far the infection has spread. If your child is allergic to penicillin then an alternative (but equally effective) anti-biotic is available.

Make sure your child takes the *entire course* of the medicine prescribed – don't stop half-way just because the infection is clearing.

Eyelid inflammation See *blepharitis*.

Folliculitis

This is a mild infection of the hair follicles. As this is predominantly a problem for more hairy individuals, folliculitis is not very common in children. The actual infection shows as small, yellow-headed pimples on hairy areas. Treatment involves washing the affected skin with an antiseptic solution and taking a course of antibiotics in tablet form at the same time. Folliculitis is more of a nuisance in hot climates and in those who have to wear heavy clothing.

Fungal rashes See *ringworm*.

Furuncles See *Boils*.

German measles See *rubella*.

Haemangiomata

This is a medical label for particular types of *birth mark*, those types known as *cavernous* or *strawberry haemangioma*. In these types a raised, strawberry-coloured skin mass is present on the skin. The mass can be small or large, and affect any area of the body, but is most commonly found on the head or neck. It increases in size during the first year of life and then remains constant until about seven years of age when it may disappear spontaneously. When these masses do spontaneously resolve the affected area is usually pale and flat.

Haemangiomata are often large and unsightly, causing distress to parents but little bother to the child. Their big problem is that the swelling contains masses of tiny blood vessels which bleed profusely when cut. In addition, the base of the swelling is firmly anchored to the underlying skin with tiny blood vessels so that any attempt at removal will cause heavy bleeding and result in unsightly scarring.

The traditional approach to date has been to leave the swelling alone and allow it to settle in its own time. While this is fine for some haemangiomata, others, because of their size or position, need a more aggressive approach.

The modern approach is to use *cryotherapy* – a technique explained in detail in Appendix 3. Briefly, it involves the use of intense cold to destroy tissue without resorting to surgery. In simple terms, a hollow brass probe – of varying size, depending on the area being treated – has liquid nitrogen pumped through it under pressure. As the gas flows through the probe it is cooled to as low as −200°C. An adhesive gel, lightly rubbed onto the haemangioma, acts as a medium so that the cooling probe sticks firmly to the surface. As soon as contact is established the liquid nitrogen is continually pumped ensuring an even temperature in the probe. With the probe constantly at −200°C and firmly stuck to the haemangioma, its blood vessels and tissue become totally frozen − in fact they are converted to an ice-ball. This process continues until all of the haemangioma is frozen, then the gas is turned off and the probe removed.

The blood vessels and tissues are effectively destroyed by this technique and begin to go through a series of changes, the end result of which is that the haemangioma collapses and shrivels. In other words, the bulk of the haemangioma is dramatically reduced and further freezing can be employed to produce a final result which is cosmetically more attractive than before. The beauty of this technique is that no surgery is involved and consequently the blood vessels never bleed −they just collapse.

Cryosurgery is relatively new in Britain and Ireland but widely used in the USA, where the process has been tried and refined over a 20-year period.

Hand, foot and mouth disease

This is a blistering condition of the palms of the hand, soles of the feet and inside of the mouth. It is caused by a virus called *coxsackie* (don't let that label worry you − it's just a name for a virus to distinguish it from others). The blisters erupt in small numbers over a few days and may cover the affected areas very quickly in some cases. The virus is easily passed on and the condition often occurs in epidemics.

If your child develops this problem he/she may be off-colour and have a slight fever. The blisters inside the mouth will be a nuisance because of pain and discomfort, but always heal without damage.

There is no treatment apart from occasional mouthwashes and pain-killers. The rash usually fades within ten days. There is absolutely no connection between this condition and the foot and mouth disease of animals. In each condition there are blisters on the described areas but the animal strain is caused by a completely different 'bug' and cannot be passed to humans. Equally, the human strain is not transmitted to animals.

Heat rash

This is a red, itchy rash with pimples and blisters at the openings of sweat glands, and is also called *prickly heat*. The rash is particularly present on the face, neck, shoulders and chest where the sweat glands are concentrated. It can also erupt on the inside of joints, for example in the creases of the groin, when the term *intertrigo* may be used as a description. The rash occurs when the skin overheats and reacts with a mild inflammation. The rash is invariably itchy and, if left unchecked, can become infected.

Management is directed mainly at removing the underlying cause: keep the child cool and dry and remove any clothing which doesn't allow air to circulate, such as plastic nappy covers. No wool or nylon should be next to the skin as these irritate. A mild hydrocortisone-based cream will produce a quick resolution to the rash but a simple moisturizer (see Appendix 1 for details) will probably be just as effective. Rub it in two or three times daily. Do not use dusting powders as they only block the pores, cake the skin and interfere with the natural healing process.

Herpes

This is the name given to a virus which has a habit of causing skin problems in children. There are three important types of herpes infection that may become a nuisance to your child:

Herpes simplex

Commonly called *cold sores* – but the herpes virus does not cause the common cold. This infection produces red, blistering itchy and sore rashes on the lips. The first infection occurs in infancy – for instance after being kissed by a person with an active infection – and the virus passes through the skin, travels up a nerve and 'hides' in the nerve root until reactivated. Reactivation can be provoked by colds, flu, tummy upsets, fatigue, stress, local injury, bright sunlight or even a strong wind blowing onto the skin surface. Once reactivated the virus travels from the nerve root back down to the skin surface producing the eruption known as cold sores. There are four stages to the eruption:

- *Tingle stage.* At this stage most children know they are about to get a cold sore. The skin tingles and itches before the sore appears.
- *Blister stage.* This stage begins as a small, raised blotch which swells and forms blisters, either singly or in small clusters. The blisters are often very painful.

46

- *Weeping stage*. Many children find this stage the most embarrassing and unsightly. The blisters collapse and join up to form a large, weeping sore. The virus can easily be spread to other people at this time.
- *Scab stage*. The blisters begin to dry out and heal. A scab begins to form. If licked, the scab will crack and bleed. This stage is most vulnerable to meddling fingers – which can themselves become infected and infect other areas, as well as infecting the cold sore with other germs.

The virus is capable of infecting other parts of the body. If your child picks at the sores and then rubs his/her eyes an infection can develop there as well. Similarly if your child kisses a younger brother or sister the infection can be spread. Most importantly, if your child has **atopic eczema** and develops cold sores which seem to be spreading then have him/her checked by your doctor. If your child has cold sores and usually plays with friends who have **atopic eczema**, then keep him/her away until the cold sores have completely cleared.

The treatment of herpes simplex is as follows:

- In mild cases, dab a simple astringent such as 70% alcohol or eau de Cologne onto the affected area every two or three hours until the scab stage is reached.
- For more troublesome or recurrent cases use one of the following medications: *Herpid* (*idoxuridine 5%*), applied as soon as the first tingling symptoms are felt – this is in a paint solution and should be applied liberally every four hours for the first four days of the attack; or *Zovirax* (*acylovir*) cream, applied five times daily at four-hourly intervals for five days – ideally this should be applied as soon as the first symptoms appear.

There are no side-effects to these two preparations but they are expensive. A cheaper and more convenient treatment is to apply cold coffee to the affected area. This is a remedy found by accident to work in some sufferers and has been passed around by word of mouth. It does indeed work for many people and is useful in an emergency if your doctor is unavailable. The coffee is applied on a piece of cotton wool every two or three hours and left to dry.

It will help in isolating the infection and preventing it from spreading if you observe one or two points of hygiene. Avoid sharing eating and drinking utensils and towels with a child if he/she has cold sores, and always wash your hands after touching the cold sores, for example, when applying medication to them.

One final point – if the cold sores seem to be spreading towards the eye or if one eye becomes red and sore during a bout of cold sores then have your doctor assess the situation as the virus may be in the eye as well as on the skin.

Herpes stomatitis

This is a common and very unpleasant children's illness for which much is prescribed but with few benefits. It is very much a case of nature producing the best cure – even if it seems a bit slow. The healing process rarely proceeds with any problems.

A child with herpes stomatitis is feverish and looks unwell. He/she will drool excessively. All attempts at feeding are resisted and the reason is soon obvious – the inside of the mouth, cheeks, gums and tongue are covered in small painful ulcers. The ulcers start slowly and become established over about three days before eventually healing. However, during this time the mouth is extremely sore and the child finds feeding too painful. The time from eruption to healing is about five to seven days. The only treatment likely to work in this condition is called *Zovirax* (the chemical name is *acyclovir*) which is available as an oral suspension. The dosage is 2½ ml five times daily for children under two years of age and 5 ml five times daily for children over two years of age.

Because of the distressing nature of this condition a lot of love and comfort is needed – jelly and ice-cream are useful sources of nutrition and all drinks should be cool.

The following *do not help* – antibiotics, anti-fungals, antiseptic mouthwashes. Some local anaesthetic mouthwashes may be tried but their usefulness is doubtful.

Herpes zoster

This infection is more commonly known as *shingles*, and the virus involved is the one which causes *chicken-pox*. Consequently there are two variations of infection from the same 'bug'.

Shingles is a skin inflammation over one (or more) nerves in the body. In other words the inflammation follows the pathway of the underlying nerve – sometimes along its full extent. The appearance of the skin rash is often preceded by pain or itching over the affected area and occasionally the pain persists for some time after the rash has gone. The shingles infection can damage the underlying nerve for a short period, leaving it weakened. However, in time it will usually be restored to normal. Shingles is a red, blistering rash in which the blisters appear to follow a definite line. For as long as the rash is present it is important to follow a few simple guidelines: keep the area clean and dry, and use only prescribed lotions directly on the inflamed skin. The two most likely prescribed preparations are Herplex-D and Zovirax (see *herpes simplex*).

Hives See *urticaria*.

Impetigo

Commonly known as *school sores*, this is a particularly troublesome skin infection caused by a specific bacteria called *Staphylococcus aureus*. The face is the area most frequently affected but other areas can be troubled as well. The rash looks like crusty red sores which the child may pick at and consequently spread the infection. Impetigo may result from poorly managed *eczema* where the inflamed skin acts as a source of nutrients for passing bacteria. Impetigo may also result from the scratching associated with certain infestations such as *scabies* (see also *pediculosis*).

The usual treatment involves soaking the infected area with an antiseptic solution followed by the application of an antibiotic cream. Occasionally oral antibiotics are necessary for extensive areas or in order to clear the infection more quickly. While the child has active infected sores the potential for spreading the infection to others exists – consequently it would be prudent to keep your child away from others until the problem has cleared totally.

Infantile acne See *acne vulgaris*.

Infantile eczema See *atopic eczema*.

Infestation See *pediculosis*; *scabies*.

Intertrigo See *heat rash*.

Insect bites See *papular urticaria*.

Juvenile plantar dermatosis

This long medical phrase describes something quite simple – an inflammation of the skin on the feet, usually occurring in children and young teenagers. It is quite a common problem and becoming more troublesome recently as footwear manufacturers introduce new linings

49

to the soles and sides of shoes. If the child's feet sweat there is a contact reaction between the sweat, the shoe lining and the feet producing an inflammation (see Chapter 1). Left unchecked, the child's feet become red, sore and blister. The condition is treated by applying a cortisone cream of appropriate strength (see Appendix 1 for details) and the removal (or covering up) of the offending shoe lining. Ideally the child should wear cotton socks, regularly changed, and avoid direct skin contact with shoe linings.

Keloid

This medical label describes an unsightly scarring effect where the skin heals to produce a thick swelling instead of the usual edge-to-edge join. It can result from surgery or trauma such as a cut from a fall. Keloids are commonest in black children. The recognition of keloid formation is important (cosmetically only) in that any form of surgery or cuts/lacerations will almost certainly heal in a similar fashion. Equally the keloid cannot be removed surgically as the resulting heal is likely to be similarly affected. One treatment used is the injection of a long-acting cortisone drug (see Appendix 1 for details) directly into the keloid. This tends to shrink the thickened skin and produce a more acceptable scar.

Keratosis pilaris

This is a patchy roughness of the skin, particularly over the back of the upper arms and the front of thighs. It is due to a plugging of the hair follicles, causing the surrounding skin to bulge out slightly and appear rough. There is no real treatment apart from moisturizers for very rough areas and there is no real (or important) cause. Children with this condition tend to grow out of it at puberty.

Lip-licking

This is a red, crusty rash around the lips caused by repeatedly licking the area. This is more often a problem for children with dry skin conditions such as *eczema*. The rash is fairly easily identified as it does not spread beyond the length of the tongue and the child can be seen to repeatedly lick the affected area regularly.

Obviously any healing with be difficult for as long as the area is continually licked. A very mild 1% hydrocortisone ointment is used to induce a resolution of the rash and the child encouraged to apply the ointment every time he/she feels like licking – even if this means a dozen times daily (you cannot damage the skin with this strength of cream). Once the skin has healed and the child stopped licking, the condition disappears.

Measles

This is a highly contagious viral condition with severe catarrhal symptoms affecting the eyes, nose and chest. There is an associated blotchy red rash that starts behind the ears but spreads over the face and body. Tiny white spots (koplik spots) can be seen on the inside of the cheeks. At first the child may seem only to have a heavy cold with fever, aching limbs and streaming nose. Eventually the full-blown eye, nose and chest symptoms appear, with the rash erupting after about four days. The virus incubates for about ten days before the onset of symptoms and the child is infectious for approximately five days before and after the rash appears.

The management of measles is mainly supportive as viral illnesses must run their course. Bed rest in a darkened room, plenty of fluids and lots of cuddles are the order of the day. Antibiotics are reserved for bacterial infections on top of the underlying measles.

There is a vaccination programme in most countries nowadays to prevent measles erupting in children. The vaccine is given after twelve months of age.

Miliaria

These are small white pimples appearing on the face, nose and mouth of new-born babies. They have a red base and are only occasionally seen on the body. They are commonly referred to as 'milk spots'. There is no treatment, the spots have no significance and usually fade within a few weeks.

Moles

These are brown, brownish-black or bluish-black skin patches of varying sizes. Their medical significance is related to their simple cosmetic/nuisance value and the fact that they can potentially turn into skin cancers.

In children, moles can be divided into those occurring at or within a few weeks of life (*congenital moles*) and those occurring some time after birth, usually after puberty (*acquired moles*). There is a very rare and dreadfully disfiguring congenital mole called a *giant congenital naevus* where the newborn skin is partly covered in a blackish skin layer which does look horrible. This type of mole is very rare but very important as it has a high chance of turning cancerous.

A smaller form of this last type (*small congenital naevus*) occurs in about 1% of white children. It appears within six weeks of birth and persists throughout life. Small congenital naevi vary in size and quite often have coarse hairs growing from them. They have a very remote possibility of turning cancerous.

The majority of moles on children are called *benign pigmented naevi*, reflecting the fact that they rarely turn cancerous and are obvious by virtue of the pigment in the skin. They can be brown, brownish-black or bluish-black.

Leaving aside the giant congenital mole, which is a rarity requiring special treatment, any mole can be removed. Whether or not it should be, however, depends, first, on whether it shows signs of turning cancerous, and second, on its appearance and location – the removal of an unsightly mole, or of one which is in an awkward position, such as behind a bra-strap, is probably justified. Removal is also recommended for moles on the palms of hands, soles of feet, and on genitalia. It is also common practice to remove moles on sites of constant friction such as the beard area and waistline because the irritation might encourage cancerous change.

Removal involves one of two methods: *surgical excision*, where the mole and a small amount of surrounding skin is cut out with a scalpel and the resulting gap stitched together; or *cryosurgery* – an intense freezing technique where the mole is effectively destroyed and separated from its base. Cryosurgery is explained in detail in Appendix 3 but, briefly, it involves the use of liquid nitrogen driven through a small brass tip. As the gas rushes through the hollow tip it is frozen to $-200°C$. If the tip is held against skin it immediately sticks and produces a localized frost bite. Nature then separates the frozen tissue over the ensuing weeks, and the area heals without leaving a scar. Cryosurgery can reduce the size of bulky, hairy moles to normal skin level and makes their colour less unattractive. Depending on the final cosmetic result required the freezing technique can be repeated to leave the skin with a more acceptable appearance.

If you are worried about moles on your child and their potential for cancerous change then ask yourself the following questions:

1. Does the mole itch (is your child scratching it)?
2. Is the size greater than ½ in/1 cm in diameter?
3. Is the mole getter bigger?

4. Is the mole irregular in outline?
5. Is the mole becoming very dark or black?
6. Does the mole appear inflamed?
7. Is the mole bleeding or crusting?

If you answered YES to two or more questions you should have the mole checked by your doctor. If you answered YES only once or not at all it is very, very unlikely that the moles you are worried about are becoming cancerous. It is recommended that you reassess any moles your child has by asking the above seven questions at least once each year. An increasing score suggests medical attention is required to ensure all is well.

Molluscum contagiosum

This is a *wart*-like skin problem in which small eruptions appear on the skin in clusters. They are particularly troublesome in children with *atopic eczema*, in whom the eruptions may spread quickly. If squeezed, a cheese-like material is produced which is quite infectious and contains the virus responsible for the rash.

There are two main methods of dealing with molluscum contagiosum: *cryotherapy* (see Appendix 3) where the areas are individually frozen causing the eruption to fall off within days leaving no scar; or by 'spiking' each eruption with a sharpened orange stick dipped in liquid phenol. This effectively destroys the eruption. My own preference is to use cryotherapy as there is less pain, a better success rate and more acceptable cosmetic end result.

Monilia See *Candida*.

Mouth ulcers

These are small erosions affecting the inside lining of the mouth. The ulcers are very painful and may produce an irritable unhappy child for as long as they are present. In one condition, *herpes stomatitis*, the mouth is covered in ulcers for a few days and is associated with general malaise and fever.

Some children experience recurring or persisting mouth ulcers and recent evidence suggests there may be a dietary link in such cases. Before putting your child on any diet do check with your doctor to ensure this is the correct approach. As a guideline, if your child experiences recurring or persisting mouth ulcers for as much as three months in a year then look at diets which are free of dairy products, artificial colouring or preservatives, or gluten (see Appendix 4).

The many other treatments for mouth ulcers involve soothing mouthwashes and cortisone-based tablets held against the ulcer. In my opinion they are of little value, but worth a try at least once.

Naevus. See *moles*.

Napkin dermatitis

This is the medical name for *nappy rash*. Your baby's skin is thinner than an adult's and, therefore, much more susceptible to becoming inflamed by infection or irritants. Prolonged contact with urine or faeces, softening of the skin induced by wet napkins and waterproof pants can bring on this type of skin inflammation which doctors call a *contact eczema* and the inflamed skin is easily infected.

Nappy rashes are best managed by keeping the area clean and dry by avoiding heavy dressings. Plastic or rubber pants should not be used except for important occasions. Disposable napkins are preferable to those which require plastic overpants. Towelling nappies are best if thoroughly washed, rinsed and sterilized. A mild detergent is advisable and the washing machine rinse cycle needs to be completed twice. The napkins can be sterilized by soaking them in a chlorinated isocyanurate solution. Nappies must be changed often.

If treatment is needed use strictly as prescribed and do not overuse to try and get quicker results. If there is a mild eruption with even a little ulceration of the skin then simple treatment will be sufficient, such as titanium dioxide paste BP 50% with emulsifying ointment 50% (available from your chemist). If the area is very red and has pinpoint areas of spread then possibly a *candida* infection is occurring – this is a commonplace 'bug' which quickly settles on damaged skin surfaces and is frequently troublesome in nappy rashes. This is treated with Nystaform HC 0.5% – a weak hydrocortisone/anti-thrush preparation. When the rash has settled a barrier preparation such as zinc and castor-oil ointment should be applied with each nappy change to prevent recurrence, taking care to cover the 'creases' in your baby's skin.

Napkin psoriasis

This can begin in the first week of life, often starting as thick *crusting* on the scalp. An inflamed, scaly rash appears on the eyebrows, behind the ears, on the neck, armpits and groin. The nappy area is almost always involved, with a circular, scaly red rash which resembles *psoriasis*.

Because nappies don't allow air to circulate, the skin will look red and glazed. While alarming to the parents, this causes no real distress to the child. Once cleared, the long-term outlook for the child is excellent although there is a suspicious link between this condition in infancy and the development of either *eczema* or *psoriasis* later in life.

The rash can be treated as follows:

- Bathe your child daily in an emollient bath such as silcox base (see Chapter 3 for details).
- Use a combination mild hydrocortisone/anti-fungal cream to all affected areas except the face and scalp. This is because the *candida* 'bug' often settles on the inflamed skin. The cream can only be obtained on prescription from your doctor.
- Apply 1% hydrocortisone cream to face and ear creases three or four times daily.
- Apply warmed olive oil to the scalp to remove adherent scale. If this does not do the job then 1% salicylic acid ointment (available from your doctor) can be used daily and washed out with a simple shampoo.

Nappy rash. See *napkin dermatitis*.

Nettle rash. See *urticaria*.

Nits. See *pediculosis capitis*.

Papular urticaria

This is the medical term for an overreaction in the skin to insect bites. Characteristically crops of blistering eruptions occur on the trunk and limbs, which are intensely itchy. Children affected will scratch the areas vigorously, leading to further skin damage and often an infection settling on top of the damaged skin. Occasionally the condition will last for years, on and off, worsening in warm weather. The insects involved are *fleas*, *mosquitoes*, *sand flies* and *grass mites*. Children new to a particular area where such insects are abundant are particularly at risk.

The management of the condition involves identifying where the insects are being harboured and using a suitable pesticide there. All pets should be carefully screened and treated. A flea collar should be used on any animals that the child is likely to come into contact with. Pesticides should also be applied to bedding, furniture and the outside inch of fitted carpets. The child will usually get relief from an *antihistamine* tablet (see Chapter 3 for details) and a local cream to soothe the itchy skin. Any infection of the skin will need to be treated with an appropriate *antibiotic* cream.

Paronychia

This is an infection of the nail fold and occurs frequently in children who bite their nails and damage the cuticle sufficiently to allow bugs to get into the less protected areas. There are two forms – *acute* and *chronic*.

Acute paronychia is characterized by redness, swelling, tenderness and pain around the nail fold, caused by a bacterium known as *Staphylococcus aureus*. When this occurs the infection needs to be opened and the build-up of pus drained away. Your family doctor should be able to perform this simple surgical procedure. Your child will also need to be put on an appropriate antibiotic.

In chronic paronychia a low-grade but persistent infection is present in the nail fold causing redness, swelling and mild discomfort. This is most commonly the result of frequently immersing the hands in water and I have seen it in children who swim regularly and for long periods. Left unchecked the nail becomes badly disfigured as any growth in the nail is damaged by the infection.

The commonest infecting 'bugs' are *candida*, *ringworm*, and a bacterium called *pseudomonas*. This latter 'bug' tends to produce a greenish discoloration of the nail fold.

Mangement involves killing the infection and paying attention to the precipitating factors such as regular immersion in water. Special anti-fungal creams (see Appendix 2 for details) massaged into the nail folds three or four times daily for six to 12 weeks will eventually kill candida or ringworm. After this a preparation such as 3% thymol in chloroform or 15% sulphacetamide in 50% alcohol applied to the nail folds three times daily will inhibit further infection and prevent unsightly discoloration in the developing nail plate.

For resistant cases then anti-fungal tablets may need to be taken: occasionally the nail has to be removed totally and the nail bed aggressively treated as above to allow a new, healthier, nail to grow.

Pediculosis

This is an infestation, mainly of the hairy areas of the body by a 'bug' called *Pediculus humanus* which is a louse. The lice are blood-sucking, wingless insects which use human blood as their source of nutrition and obtain it by thrusting a pair of sharp antennae into the skin and causing minute cuts. Saliva is then injected from the insect into the skin and this produces the itch. In heavily infested areas several hundred bites are inflicted daily and produce reactions ranging from redness through to heavily scratched and thickened skin. The female louse is fertilized five or six times daily and lays eggs which she firmly cements to hair shafts. When an egg hatches the empty eggshell (called a *nit*) remains attached to the hair.

Transmission of lice is by close contact and this is thought to explain why they are so common in children who make frequent contact during play. Some forms of lice can be picked up by sleeping in infested bedclothes. The various areas of the body of possible infestation have different names and treatments:

Pediculosis capitis

This is the name for an infestation by *head lice*. These should be treated with a special shampoo (containing *lindane*). The hair should be cropped short. The shampoo is then used again seven to ten days later and the hair finely combed in order to totally eradicate the 'bugs' and their empty eggshells.

Pediculosis corporis

This refers to body lice, which are more a problem for vagabounds and derelicts. Treatment involves burning all clothing, a hot bath and a total application of a 1% lindane solution

Pediculosis pubis

This refers to lice in the pubic hair area. These are usually discovered after scratching an itch in the area. Intimate body contact (such as sexual activity) are the commonest ways of acquiring these lice but they can also be picked up from towels and beds. The same shampoo containing lindane will get rid of pubic lice, but all bedlinen and towels should be hot laundered to kill off any remaining lice.

Peri-oral dermatitis. See **lip-licking**.

Pityriasis rosea

This is a self-limiting eruption of a reddish circular disc-like rash on the body and limbs. It is quite often preceded by a solitary circular area which may appear anywhere on the trunk but usually the chest. Within ten days of this simple eruption other areas of the body, except (usually) for the neck, forearms and lower legs, are seen to be affected.

The eruptions are reddish-pink, scaly and mildly itchy. The rash may last for up to eight weeks, fading in some areas as it appears in others. In severe cases the rash may affect the hands and feet, be extremely itchy and last for about three months.

There is no known cause for this condition but suspicions rest on an infecting 'bug' (yet to be isolated) or a reaction to certain medicines.

Since the rash clears spontaneously and usually quite quickly the need for treatment is minimal. Mild moisturizers twice daily with a soap substitute may help and for very itchy troublesome areas, one of the cortisone creams (see Appendix 1 for details) is useful. Sunlight is also very beneficial (when you can get it!) Bear in mind, though, that the rash will fade in time, leaving no residual problems.

Pityriasis versicolor

This is a superficial infection of the skin by a *yeast* 'bug' (see Chapter 1) producing slightly scaly patches of depigmentation of the body, varying in size and often merging with each other. The usual areas of infection are the back, chest, upper arms, neck and face. The affected places are more apparent with suntanning. On untanned skin the infection appears brownish in colour. Sometimes the infection is confirmed by examining the skin under a microscope and observing the yeast 'bug'. More often than not the diagnosis is made by simple observation.

There may be a connection between some suntan lotions and the emergence of this infection (or least its tendency to recur). This is especially true of lotions containing coconut oil. If your child has or has had, this type of infection you should avoid coconut-oil suntan lotions.

The management of this infection involves killing off the yeast 'bug' and allowing the skin to return to normal. The simplest, safest and cheapest treatment is to apply selenium sulphide shampoo (Selsun) – lathered over the head and trunk and left to dry overnight. It is rinsed off the next morning. This procedure must be carried out on three consecutive nights. There are anti-fungal creams and tablets (see Appendix 2 for details) available for severe or resistant cases.

Pompholyx

These are large blisters on the hands or feet in association with a **contact eczema** reaction. The blisters are usually ruptured under clean conditions, followed by soaking in a tepid 1:10,000 potassium permanganate solution and wet dressings of 0.5% silver nitrate, which soothe the skin. If an infection is present then oral antibiotics are often required. For further details on treatment, see **contact eczema**.

Prickly heat. See ***heat rash.***

Psoriasis

Of all the skin conditions likely to affect your child, next to ***atopic eczema***, this is the most frustrating and troublesome. It is frustrating in that doctors do not fully understand what causes it (though it is known that it is *not* caught from animals, that it is not caused by dirt or stress,though stress, sudden shock, emotional upsets or excitement can cause flare-ups, and that some infections, such as tonsilitis, can trigger it).

It is troublesome in that time, perseverance and patience are terribly important in beating it. There is *no* cure (though the pharmaceutical companies are confident that a cure is not far away), none of the alternative medical therapies, such as acupuncture and homoeopathy, will make any difference and diet similarly has no role to play. However, it can be well controlled by different treatments, so with any luck and with good care your child's skin will be clear for long periods, even years. And if one treatment doesn't work, there's a good chance that another will.

Psoriasis takes its name from the Greek word for *itch* and is a recurring or long-lasting (*chronic*) skin condition flaring up and settling down again at intervals. Healthy skin, as you saw in Chapter 1, is constantly replaced by new cells produced beneath the skin's surface – a process which takes roughly 28 days. With psoriasis, this turnover is accelerated and cells are replaced seven times as rapidly as normal – every four days. The immature cells reaching the skin's surface are not ready to be shed like older skin cells, so they stick to the skin in small, flaky, silvery mounds, giving the typical look of psoriasis. The skin can also look red and is susceptible to bleeding if scratched because the blood flow to the affected areas is increased. Sometimes psoriasis patches itch and irritate.

There is more than one type of psoriasis and the commonest are:

- Plaque, or *common psoriasis*. This most often affects the legs, lower back, knees, elbows and scalp – especially where prone to knocks and bumps – and is characterized by raised, round or oval, red plaques of affected skin which are rough to the touch and covered with silvery scales.
- *Flexural psoriasis*. This form of psoriasis affects the folds and creases of the body. The affected patches of skin are often moist rather than scaly, and can be sore. Older or overweight people are more prone to flexural psoriasis because there are more folds of skin on their bodies.

- *Guttate psoriasis*. This name – from the Latin for a 'drop' – describes a condition characterized by lots of scattered 'mini-spots' of psoriasis, most often affecting children and young teenagers. It is usually triggered by, and starting a few weeks after, a *sore throat* or *tonsillitis*.
- *Psoriasis of the nails*. This usually occurs with other types of psoriasis, but sometimes on its own. The nails look pitted or dented, change colour, thicken, or sometimes a nail becomes separated from its nail bed.

About 2% of the population suffer from psoriasis and both boys and girls are affected. Although the skin looks unsightly and embarrasing the disorder is not contagious or infectious and with proper treatment can be brought under control. It tends to run in families, although we don't yet know the reason. A parent with psoriasis has a one-in-three chance of passing it onto children. If both parents have it, the risk increases to one in two. When a twin develops psoriasis, there's a high chance – greater for identical twins – that the other twin will do so too, although not necessarily at the same age. But then, sometimes psoriasis appears from nowhere in someone with no family history.

Many parents with psoriasis feel in some way responsible if their child then develops it – as if in some way they could have prevented it, which of course they couldn't. This feeling can be difficult to deal with – thinking rationally when a child's well-being is affected is not easy. But it's not anybody's fault and blaming yourself won't help the child. In fact, if stress aggravates the psoriasis anyway, this needless soul-searching may well make it worse. If a parent is relaxed and matter-of-fact about the psoriasis, there's a good chance the child will also cope well.

A wide variety of treatments can be tried. There's a good chance that one will help your child.

- *Coal-tar treatment*. An effective way of clearing up affected skin and scalps. Applying coal-tar preparations – they come in gel, cream, ointment, bath additive and shampoo forms – used to be rather a messy, smelly business, but with most of today's newer, more refined preparations this is no longer such a problem. Names you're likely to come across include *Psoriderm*, *Gelcotar*, *Alphosyl* and *Psorigel*. Coal-tar preparations stop itching, heal and improve appearance and lessen skin thickening by reducing the high turnover of skin cells. Coal tar is usually combined with other substances like *allantoin* or *salicylic acid* which remove the scales of dead skin that adhere to psoriasis patches. Note, however, that some skins are allergic to coal tar and it sometimes causes *folliculitis*. If you notice a reaction see your GP.

- *Short contact therapy.* This is a relatively new and helpful programme, based on the use of one of the oldest treatments of all – dithranol (one brand name is Dithrocream, which comes in different strengths). Dithranol damps down the growth of cells on the epidermis (see Chapter 1) and reduces scaliness. Care is needed, however, as it can irritate and burn the skin; it should also be kept away from fabrics, plastics and certain other materials as it may cause stains. Keep it away from the mouth and eyes, and wash your hands after use.

The cream should be applied once a day and left on for only 30 minutes. It is rubbed carefully into the psoriatic areas until absorbed, taking care to avoid the surrounding skin. Wear an old dressing gown to avoid staining clothes that may be new. Wash the cream off after 30 minutes by showering or bathing, rinsing the bath or shower with hot water immediately afterwards, and using a suitable cleaner to remove any deposit on bathroom surfaces.

The treated areas of skin may gradually become stained purple or brown. This colouration is harmless, and will usually disappear within a few days at the end of the treatment. You should not attempt to scrub the colour from your child's skin.

For use on the scalp, first comb the hair to remove loose scales, and after suitably parting, rub the cream well into the affected areas, removing after 30 minutes by shampooing the hair. Blond or fair hair may take on a pinkish tinge, but this will grow out after treatment stops. This staining can be avoided by following the instructions carefully. Hairstyles which are easy to manage are a distinct advantage in psoriasis of the scalp.

Follow these routines once a day until the skin is entirely clear – it may take up to four weeks to achieve this. You must be satisfied that the texture of the affected area is normal, and that the treatment isn't causing problems on your child's 'clear' skin. If you have seen no improvement after a week, don't despair. It is possible that you need a different strength of Dithrocream, and you should go back and ask your doctor.

Don't use Dithrocream on very sore, angry-looking psoriasis. If treated areas become inflamed, reduce the frequency of application of the ointment and consult your doctor.

- *Cortisone creams.* These are easy to use with no stain or smell, and you might think they seem the obvious choice. But it is easy to overlook the fact that they're of limited long-term benefit and can

61

have side-effects, so they may not be the most suitable. Their main effect is to suppress inflammation, but they don't actually heal the skin, so soon after you stop using them, the psoriasis patches return. Cortisone creams are more and more considered to have only a small role – if any – to play in psoriasis treatments, but may be used to help out in certain situations. It is important when using cortisone creams to follow a step-ladder procedure, gradually using weaker and weaker creams in order to prevent a rebound of the condition (see Appendix 3).

For severe psoriasis there are other cortisone therapies given in injection or tablet form. However they are fairly potent and unlikely to be used for your child.

● *Light therapy*. Some children with psoriasis benefit from using an ultra-violet lamp or simply from a couple of weeks' sunshine. Occasionally the combination of plenty of sunshine and seawater at specially developed spa resorts is particularly beneficial – the Dead Sea resorts in Israel are the best known. Other areas include Lanzarote and Yugoslavia. However, remember that your child's healthy skin can get sunburnt so don't allow this treatment to create problems in addition to the one you're trying to solve.

Purpura

This is the medical term for a small *ecchymosis* or **bruise**.

Remember that children in their day-to-day activities will end up with many bumps and bruises and often the appearance of these gives rise to concern. However, in the majority of cases there is no real problem. In some children the sudden appearance of small areas of bleeding is important and may reflect a reaction to a medication recently taken. In general, if your child develops a number of small reddish blue areas under the skin surface then have him/her examined by your doctor.

One very important type of purpura is called *Henoch–Schonlein syndrome* (also called *allergic purpura*); it is characterized by a reddish rash on the fronts of the limbs and on the buttocks. This rash quickly turns dark blue, showing that it is really a collection of bleeds. There may be an associated swelling of the hands and feet with pains in the joints and abdomen.

This is a fairly serious condition, and unfortunately the cause is often hard to find, but it usually settles well in time with hospital treatment. The management, investigations and actual therapies are very detailed and beyond the scope of this book. However, the long-term outcome is usually excellent.

Ringworm

Ringworm infections produce varying types of rash on the different areas of the body affected. If the affected area is the scalp, any bald areas the child has, usually oval shaped, will be covered with dry scales and may be itchy. Closer inspection may reveal stumps of broken-off hairs among the scales. If the area affected is the body, a circular red patchy rash will develop with a slightly raised edge. This rash may be localized to one or two areas or may be spread over a much wider surface. The rash will be itchy. If it is the groin, a red rash will extend from the inside of both thighs to the groin. It will be quite itchy – especially at night – and probably will have a slightly raised edge.

The commonest form of ringworm occurs on the feet and starts as an itch in between the toes which then produces whitish, boggy-type skin which peels away easily. The itch is worst at night and the fungus is transferred from one foot to the other by rubbing the feet together to relieve the itch (see *athlete's foot*).

As with all skin infections, treatments are either local or general. Creams containing anti-fungal medicines are used for localized ringworm infections. There is a list of the many anti-ringworm creams, paints and oral tablets and suspensions in Appendix 2 but the following principles apply: ringworm localized to feet, groin and small areas of the body usually only require the regular application of an anti-fungal cream three or four times daily to promote total skin clearance. It is a good idea to continue using the cream for at least five days after the skin looks healthy again so as to ensure total eradication of the fungus.

Ringworm which is resistant to simple remedies or which is fairly widespread over the body or which involves the nails or scalp probably requires a more aggressive approach involving oral anti-fungal tablets as well as the use of creams. This is to attack the fungal rash from inside and outside the skin layer. If oral tablets are used then the usual time-scale is one month of daily treatment. For very resistant ringworm this therapy can continue for up to three months.

Rubella

This condition is also known as *German measles*. It is a mild childhood illness caused by a virus (see Chapter 1) in which the main features are swelling of the neck glands and a blotchy pale pink rash which spreads over most of the body. Some general malaise, cough, sore throat, headaches and fever may precede the swollen glands or rash. The virus is usually active in the body for up to 16 days before the symptoms begin and the child is infectious for at least seven days from the onset of the 'cold-like' symptoms. The condition is mild and requires only rest and fluids. No other treatment is required and the rash fades quickly. There are rarely any complications.

The main significance of the rubella virus is its ability to cause disastrous abnormalities in the unborn child of any pregnant woman who may catch the condition. For this reason it is prudent to keep any pregnant woman well away from your child if he/she has rubella. Nowadays, however, with so many women very much aware of rubella, most (if not all) will have been vaccinated against the condition and are therefore unlikely to 'catch' the virus even on close contact. Because old fears die hard, you might still find pregnant friends reluctant to visit if rubella is in the household.

Scabies

This is an intensely itchy, blistering rash which occurs on the hands, feet, neck, groin and body of affected children. It is due to infestation by an insect called *Sarcoptes scabiei* which burrows into the skin and lays eggs. The diagnosis is made difficult by the intense scratching damaging the skin which in turn may become infected. Quite often scabies is mistaken for infected *atopic eczema*. However, the typical body distribution (especially in the web spaces of the fingers) soon leads to the correct conclusion. Scabies can be definitely identified by examining the skin scrapings under a microscope.

There is a range of anti-scabies preparations on the market, most freely available without a prescription; e.g. (A) 1% gamma benzene hexachloride (marketed as *lindane*) with which a single head-to-toe application for between eight and 12 hours is usually sufficient. All close contacts should be treated at the same time – whether itching or not – since the mites may still be incubating. Lindane should be used carefully in small infants because of the potential for toxicity from skin absorption of the lotion. (B) 25% benzyl benzoate emulsion is also widely used. This is applied, head-to-toe, on two consecutive nights following a hot bath.

If an infection has set in on top of the scratching then an appropriate antibiotic cream may also be needed (see *impetigo*).

Scabies mites can survive for up to 36 hours away from humans – even longer in cold conditions. For this reason it is advisable to wash bedlinen and clothing in hot water and use a hot drying cycle. Clothing which cannot be washed should be dry-cleaned. There are commercially available sprays for disinfecting furniture and mattresses – ask your pharmacist for details (see also *atopic eczema* for details of house dust mite control).

Scalded skin syndrome

This is known medically as *toxic epidermal necrolysis* and is a very serious, life-threatening reaction to a skin infection. A simple *impetigo* is a skin infection caused by a bacterium called *Staphylococcus aureus*. The usual features are redness, crusting and weeping of the affected area. However, in infants and small children a more generalized reaction can occur with whole layers of skin peeling off, leaving raw, unprotected areas. The damaged patches look like red, moist, scalded skin. Because of the extent of skin shedding and the potential for heat and fluid loss, children with this condition are always hospitalized and treated with intravenous drips containing replacement fluids and protein. A very aggressive antibiotic routine is initiated at the same time and given through the drip.

In the majority of children complete and total recovery takes place, even though they are often gravely ill at the beginning of therapy.

Scarlet fever

This is a bacterial infection of the throat which causes a rash to form on the body. The first signs are those of tonsillitis, with sore throat, loss of appetite and fever. There may be accompanying stomach cramps and vomiting. Within two or three days tiny red dots appear on the skin, which has an overall red flush. The rash starts on the chest and neck, then spreads to the whole body. There are no spots or flushing around the mouth which stands out as markedly pale. When the rash fades (within a week) there is flaking of the skin.

The infecting 'bug' has the potential to spread to and damage the kidneys. For this reason your doctor will almost certainly prescribe an appropriate antibiotic and insist on a minimum of a five-day course. There are no real complications if treated properly and the rash is merely a reflection on the skin of the infecting 'bug'. No treatment is needed for the skin.

School sores See *impetigo*.

Sebaceous cyst

This is a swelling underneath the skin causing a bulge in the skin surface. The swelling is due to a small bubble full of *sebum* (the stuff you get if you squeeze pimples) This is known as a *cyst*. The cyst has the tendency to get bigger and cause the swelling to become more obvious. Because the cyst is underneath the skin and rarely bursts of its own accord, the only satisfactory method of removal is by surgery. A small incision is made on the skin surface (under local anaesthetic) and the cut continues to the depth of the cyst itself. It can then be 'shelled' out via the incision in much the same way as peas from a pod. The incision is then stitched up and allowed to heal naturally. Some children – in their teenage years – can develop more than one cyst and become thoroughly fed up. However, cysts have no medical significance other than cosmetic and rarely become infected. They can never become cancerous.

Seborrhoeic dermatitis

Also known as *seborrhoeic eczema*. This is possibly a variant of **atopic eczema**. It is a red scaly rash which forms on the eyebrows, behind the ears, in the neck folds, armpits and groin. The nappy area is almost always involved eventually as the condition quite often erupts within the first week of life. However, this condition can begin at any age in children. The rash is itchy and irritating but nothing as dramatic as that which bedevils atopic eczema sufferers. There may be heavy crusting on the scalp.

Seborrhoeic dermatitis can be cleared quickly with an aggressive, appropriate programme and the long-term outlook in such cases is excellent . It is treated as follows:

- Wash all areas carefully on a daily basis using an emollient such as silcox base (see Chapter 3 for details).
- Use a mild hydrocortisone agent combined with an anti-fungal cream to all affected areas except face and scalp. This should be applied three times daily. The anti-fungal cream is added as quite often **candida** bugs grow on top of the inflamed skin. Failure to treat these will delay healing.
- 1% hydrocortisone cream is applied three times daily to face and ears.
- Warmed olive oil is applied to the scalp scale and left on for 30 minutes. It can then be washed away with a mild, non-scented shampoo.

With regular applications of the above routine, most children's skin and scalp will quickly restore to normal and stay healthy.

Shingles See **Herpes zoster**.

Thrush See **Candida**.

Tinea

Another name for **ringworm**. There are extra Latin tags to describe the exact area of infection: *tinea capitis* affects the scalp; *tinea corporis* the trunk; *tinea cruris* the groin; and *tinea pedis* the feet (also known as *athlete's foot*).

Toxic epidermal necrolysis See *scalded skin syndrome*.

Urticaria

This is an allergic skin disorder, also known as 'hives', which appears as a blistering or wealing of the skin surface. The weals and the surrounding skin are red and there is intense itching. The weals can affect any area of the body and usually last less than 24 hours.

There are several distinct varieties of urticaria. The most common form in children, known simply as *'ordinary'* urticaria, is an allergic reaction to something the child has consumed. It may be caused by food or drugs, and it is often associated with food additives. The most common provocative foods in urticaria are eggs, milk, nuts, fish, shell-fish, yeast and strawberries. Penicillin can cause it, and aspirin, tartrazine dye and benzoate preservatives are often involved (see Appendix 4 for details).

One interesting, although confusing, problem occurs in relationship to coloured tablets used in treatment routines. If your child develops an urticarial reaction to, say a penicillin tablet with a red coating, which has caused the reaction – the penicillin or the dye used in the coating? A simple method of deciding is to wash off the outer colouring and try the tablet again. More often than not the drug can then be tolerated. This is more than just an academic exercise as it is not a good idea to have your child incorrectly labelled as allergic to penicillin, because this rules out a most important group of antibiotics useful in infectious illnesses.

The reaction usually occurs soon after the food is consumed and the child may complain of tingling inside the mouth and later develop tummy pains. There may be large, intensely itchy weals on the body, limbs and face. Quite often the child will vomit or develop diarrhoea. Because of the quick reaction involved here there is often no need to seek medical aid – the parents observe the response and learn to avoid that food in the future. Occasionally even traces of the offending foods can give problems and this needs to be noted for those occasions when the child is at parties, for example.

Contact urticaria is caused by an allergic reaction to some material which comes into direct contact with the child's skin. This causes swelling, redness and itching over the affected area. For example, some children experience this kind of reaction on their hands if they touch egg-white. The area involved swells quickly, becomes red and intensely itchy. If the child licks his/her fingers then the same response occurs on the lips and face.

This reaction can also be provoked by contact with other foods such as milk and fish, with jewellery or clothing, or by animal hair and fur, especially from cats, dogs and horses. The response to handling or stroking an animal is quite quick, and almost always confined to the area of immediate contact. Because the cause and effect are so obvious the child (or his parents) soon learn to avoid the offending materials.

The management of both contact and ordinary urticaria ideally involves the identification and removal of the provoking substance. If the child is unexpectedly exposed to one of them, the immediate treatment is mainly aimed at providing relief. A cold compress applied to the swollen, itchy areas will soothe the itching and help the swelling go down.

Your doctor will probably also prescribe an antihistamine for the itching. Antihistamines are drugs which block the effect of the hormone, histamine, which is present in higher than usual levels in the blood in urticaria. Histamine is responsible for the itch and swelling on the skin. Consequently any medicine which can block off these effects should be useful in giving your child relief. Unfortunately some antihistamines cause drowsiness and this may well become more troublesome than the itch itself. However help is at hand in the form of a new generation of antihistamines which give the relief and none of the drowsiness. In this regard Hismanal (generic name Astemizole) is probably the best of the lot. It is given in a 'loading' dose of one tablet three times daily for a few days and then once only per day after that. It is also available as a syrup.

Urticaria which lasts for more than one month is known as *chronic* urticaria, and needs careful evaluation. You should check the foods and medicines the child consumes, and notice whether the reaction occurs after contact with animals, chemicals, jewellery or clothing. You might also try the diets for urticaria given in Appendix 4.

Angio-oedema is a more dramatic-looking form of 'ordinary' urticaria, with the same causes and treatment. Angio-oedema affects the deeper skin layers, producing grossly swollen tissue. If the face is involved the features are totally distorted, with slit eyes, puffy skin and a marked itch. More often than not the rather bizarre swelling looks more dangerous than it actually is, from a medical point of view, but nevertheless still is frightening.

Only in extremely rare situations is an episode of angio-oedema actually life-threatening and this is when there is swelling inside as well as outside the throat, which narrows the wind-pipe and cuts off the air supply to the lungs. The most frequent cause of this serious reaction is a bee-sting allergy. For this reason, people at risk from such a potentially lethal allergic response carry a special injection kit containing adrenaline for self-administration if they are stung by a bee. It is beyond the scope of this book to go into the details of how and when the decisions to use this back-up treatment are made. Suffice it to say that if your child has had one episode of a dramatic reaction involving facial swelling, especially if there was any suggestion of difficulty in breathing then he/she should be seen by a specialist doctor involved in allergy – ask your family doctor for advice first.

Physical urticaria is the name given to swelling, redness and itching in response to firm pressure. In some children it is possible to 'write' on their skin by pressing with a blunt edge such as the flat end of a pencil. The weal which rises up in response to the pressure actually takes the exact shape of the letters. This is known in medical terms as *dermographism*.

A more sinister, and potentially disastrous, form of physical urticaria occurs with skin cooling. Cold water can produce a reaction on the skin which lead to a loss of consciousness. If the child is in the water and unsupervised there is a grave danger of drowning. Fortunately this is a very unusual type of urticaria, but is only ever identified by observing the reaction on the skin to cold water. If the response is serious then the child should be considered 'at risk' from total immersion in cold waters and specialist medical help sought for advice in this regard. The management of this problem is very technical and beyond the scope of this book, but suffice it to say that most children are usually cautioned strongly about swimming at all in cold waters. For the majority of children troubled by physical urticaria there is rarely the need for treatment other than a cold compress to the affected area.

Urticaria, papular See *papular urticaria*.

Verruca

This is a wart on the sole of the foot. Because of the constant pressure from walking or standing the wart tends to grow inwards (as opposed to outwards like warts on, for example, the hand). Veruccae can erupt singly or in clusters. Occasionally a group of warts forms in one area producing a patch known as a *mosaic verruca* – this will look like a swelling on the sole of the foot which, on close inspection, shows the multiple heads of individual warts. See *warts* for details on the treatment of verrucae.

Vitiligo

This is the medical term used to describe white patchy areas of the skin. The condition has no medical significance. It is due to a reduction in number or total absence of *melanocytes*, the cells needed to produce a normal skin colour, in the area of skin affected. Melanocytes also produce the darkening of the skin, called *tanning*, on exposure to sunlight. About 1% of all children will have patches of vitiligo and the only reason to cover them is for cosmetic purposes. Occasionally patches of white skin will be left after the handling of certain chemicals and may persist for years. In addition children with chronic *eczema* may find patches of vitiligo on the skin when it eventually clears. Again, the only treatment is to use cosmetic 'cover-ups'.

Warts

These are ugly skin growths caused by viral infection (see Chapter 1). The growths can be flat and red or quite large and flesh-coloured. They are easily spread and can last for many years without treatment. On occasions they disappear spontaneously.

Warts can form on the hands (usually the fingers), legs, face and genitalia. They will never become cancerous in children and their main medical significance relates to their ability to spread rapidly and their cosmetic unacceptability. They can be passed from one child to another.

Warts have their own blood supply and often have a 'root'-like base. For these reasons any removal technique must allow for the 'below the surface' beginning. A number of treatments are available:

- *Curettage*. The wart is trimmed with a blade and then 'scooped out' with an instrument called a *curette*, which is like an ice-cream scoop. This is painful, messy and leaves scarring.
- *Wart-killing creams*. A variety of creams are available commercially which, when painted onto the wart, cause the tissue to die. This routine is time-consuming and tedious. The healthy skin must be protected from the cream and the treated layers of wart removed with a blade each evening before the next layer is dealt with. Quite often the cream produces an irritant, painful reaction and the

procedure has to be abandoned. However, with perseverance and care a reasonable result is possible.

- *Cryotherapy*. This treatment, arguably the best choice for all warts, is explained in Appendix 3.

White spots on nails.

This is a fairly common phenomenon in some children and many adults and its significance is difficult to assess. There are some nutritionists who believe it reflects a low zinc level in the body, usually due to poor diet (and reflecting a high intake of junk food in particular). If your child has white spots on his or her nails it might be prudent to visit your family doctor who can decide whether a blood test for zinc deficiency is necessary.

3

Treating skin disorders

In treating your child's skin problems, there is a vast array of medications your doctor can choose from to produce a cure. Which treatment he/she decides to use depends on the condition, how long it has been present, how widespread it is and whether there are complications. For example, treating a child with a simple nappy rash can be complicated by an infection seen to be developing on top of the skin inflammation. In this situation both the infection *and* the inflammation must be dealt with if the skin is to heal. In most cases of skin disorders something is likely to be applied directly onto the damaged or diseased skin. In this chapter we look at those treatments which are prescribed.

All treatments applied to diseased skin have two components: a base (the semi-fluid substance in which the medication is mixed) and the active medication itself. Bases may be inert, simply transporting the active ingredients to the site of treatment or they may act in combination with the medication contained in them.

All bases contain combinations of the following basic ingredients:

- Powders, such as zinc oxide and calamine.
- Liquids, such as water or alcohol
- Oils and greases, such as lanolin.

The end result is a treatment in one of the following forms:

- *Lotion*. This is a suspension of insoluble powder in water. It evaporates and deposits the powder on the skin. One example is calamine lotion.
- *Cream*. This is the commonest type prescribed. All creams contain preservatives to prevent the growth of bacteria and fungi in the cream itself. Occasionally the preservatives actually produce an *allergic contact eczema*, thus defeating the purpose of the treatment. Cortisone (steroid) medications (see Appendix 1) are usually mixed in cream preparations.
- *Ointment*. This is thicker than cream and leaves the skin feeling greasy when applied. Ointments contain no water and form a protective layer over the skin, thus increasing the penetration of active constituents.
- *Paste*. This is a mixture of powder in an ointment base. Pastes

cannot be washed off with soap and water. They should be removed with cotton wool balls soaked in nut oil. Stockinette suiting or a pair of old pyjamas should be worn to protect clothing.

Once your doctor has decided on one of the above forms of treatment, he has to select the appropriate medication for the specific condition. The following are the most commonly prescribed active ingredients:

- *Cortisone (steroid)*. This is a hormone which occurs naturally in all of us, and which can be manufactured artificially. Cortisone preparations are usually used to promote healing by reducing inflammation (as for example, in *eczema*). It is prescribed in many different strengths, either as an ointment or a cream. What type of base is used is important; for example, dry, eczematous skin fares better with an ointment. Creams are slightly less effective 'carriers' of cortisone but as they disappear quickly when rubbed in there is a greater preference for them among parents. In highly resistant cases absorption of cortisone into the diseased skin can be increased by covering the affected area with polythene – polythene gloves can be worn on the hands or polythene bags on the feet – for several consecutive nights. Cortisone preparations can be combined with *antibiotics* or *antiseptics* for infected, inflamed skin conditions.
- *Antibiotics*. These are extremely useful in promoting quick healing where a skin infection exists, and does away with the need for tablets or injections.
- *Anti-viral drugs*. These are useful for *herpes* skin infections.
- *Anti-fungal drugs*. These are used in such infections as *thrush*, *athlete's foot* and *ringworm*.
- *Tars*. These are products resulting from the destructive distillation of wood or coal. They have been used successfully in the treatment of *eczema* and *psoriasis* for years. Many different preparations are available, such as strong coal-tar solution – a filtered alcoholic solution of coal tar which is incorporated into many tar pastes and ointments; proprietary preparations, such as Polytar liquid; and crude coal tar – a black, viscous liquid which can be painted on to resistant areas of *psoriasis*. Refined coal-tar preparations have a marked anti-itch and anti-psoriasis effect. Resistant *atopic eczema* which has not responded to cortisone creams occasionally responds dramatically to tar. The more 'crude' the tar preparation the more effective, and a crude tar is occasionally employed in the treatment of thickened, irritable patches of *eczema* or *psoriasis*.
- *Dithranol*. This substance is the corner-stone of the treatment of

chronic psoriasis. It is usually applied to the skin suspended in a special base known as *Lassar's paste*. Dithranol can produce a very irritating skin inflammation and eye inflammation – for these reasons it should not be applied onto the face or onto the creases of the elbows or legs. It stains clothing and turns normal skin a characteristic purple-brown which is a useful guide for doctors that the therapy is being applied! This remains for about three days after the treatment is discontinued.

- *Phenol*. In a 1% or 2% concentration in a suitable base, this is mildly *antiseptic* and *anti-itch*. It is used undiluted to treat *warts* and *molluscum contagiosum*. It is extremely caustic and must be handled with care.
- *Retinoic acid*. This is a derivative of vitamin A used in some acne treatments. It tends to cause a reddening of the face.
- *Salicylic acid*. This is a common component of pastes and ointments. It is very useful in softening scales and hard skin. As a 1% or 2% concentration in an ointment base, it is useful in *seborrhoeic eczema*. As a 10–25% concentration in a different base it can be used to treat *verrucae*.
- *Sulphur*. This is often combined with salicylic acid for scale conditions of the skin.
- *Benzoyl peroxide*. This is an antiseptic widely available as an acne preparation. It is effective but can cause reddening of the skin.
- *Moisturizers*. Quite often your family doctor or skin specialist will recommend a moisturizer to restore the skin surface to normal, if dry, or to act as a combination barrier/moisturizer. When choosing a moisturizer always go for *simple*, *non-scented* brands. Look out for the following: aqueous cream BP; E45 cream (from Boots the Chemist); emulsifying ointment BP; emollient oilatum and such branded products as Aquadrate, Calmurid, Naturderm, and Unguentum Merck.
- *Soap substitutes*. These are very useful in some long-term conditions such as *eczema* because ordinary soaps have a drying effect on the skin. A useful soap substitute is oilatum emollient: add 5–15 ml to the bath and let the child soak for 10 minutes, or apply a small amount directly to the skin, rub in, then rinse and dry. Another moisturizer/soap substitute is silcox base.
- *Antiseptic preparations*. Occasionally when some types of skin infection are present an antiseptic lotion will speed up recovery and allow for less prescribed medication to be applied. There is a wide range of antiseptics but three useful, well known, preparations are:

Gentian violet – a deep-purple-coloured liquid which kills *bacteria* and *candida*, and also helps reduce inflammation. It is often used for candida infections of the mouth and nappy areas. However, it stains the skin and clothes and for this reason is not always welcomed –even when seen to be effective.

Potassium permanganate – a lukewarm solution of potassium permanganate is helpful in acute weeping and blistering conditions particularly of the hands and feet, as may occur in contact *eczema* or *fungal* infections. The affected part is immersed for 15 minutes four times daily until healing occurs. The healing process may be speeded up by combining this treatment with a mild cortisone cream (see Appendix 1). Potassium permanganate stains the skin purple.

Cetrimide – an ammonium compound with a detergent and mild antiseptic action. Cetrimide solution BP contains 1% cetrimide with colouring and perfume for a more commercially attractive product.

- *Antihistamines*. These are medicines which block the effect of a hormone called *histamine* when released in the skin. It causes an intense itch. There are a wide variety of *antihistamines* but the safest and most effective are Triludan (terfenadine) and Hismanal (astemizole), which are sold as syrups and tablets.

Here are a few final words of advice on the use of treatments prescribed for your child:

- Listen to your doctor's advice and follow his instructions.
- Use *only* those preparations prescribed for your child. Using those prescribed for someone else could be very dangerous.
- Remember that in many long-term conditions (such as *eczema*) there are often two phases of treatment; dealing with the flare-up and then maintaining the improvement. If maintenance treatment is necessary then proper attention paid to it will prevent flare-ups.
- Do not treat cortisone (steroid) treatments as though you are handling nuclear waste. Used sensibly and correctly, they work wonders and are totally safe. Do not dab a tiny bit on and then spend five minutes trying to rub if off again – cover the affected area with a well-rubbed-in squeeze of cream. Use enough to cover the entire affected area – you will be surprised how little cream you will use.
- After opening any skin preparation keep the lid firmly closed between applications. Discard any preparations after use if specially made up. Tubes of creams or ointments should be discarded within six months of opening.

- Listen to your child and trust any complaint he/she may have about the treatment as it could be important in reporting side-effects.
- Do *not* impose silly alternative medicine therapies on your child – if you are unhappy at any particular treatment discuss it with your doctor or ask for a specialist referral. Do *not* abandon sensible orthodox treatments in the hope that some magic folk remedy will work better.
- Finish all treatments as prescribed before deciding that the results are good, bad or indifferent.
- Remember – any decision you make on your child's behalf should be sensible, safe and likely to help (rather than hinder) recovery. Your child has no way of defending him/herself against bad decisions. Trust your doctor – if you do not, then find one in whom you have confidence. You child's well-being is more important than a dent in someone's ego!

4

Questions and Answers

Quite often when you go to the family doctor or the busy clinics at many hospitals you will come away armed with a prescription, a long-winded diagnosis, a headache and a lot of questions unasked or unanswered! The following are the most commonly asked queries relating to childrens' skin disorders and the type of replies you are likely to get. Individual conditions are dealt with in Chapter 2.

Q *Are cortisone creams safe?*
A Yes. The correct and logical use of cortisone-based creams is safe, effective and promotes speedy healing. Many children are denied a resolution to skin problems because of their parents' fears of cortisone preparations. The longer the skin is left untreated the greater the chance of complications such as infection. In addition your child is denied relief from often dreadful itches and pain. There are side-effects associated with some cortisone preparations if incorrectly used (see Appendix 1) but if you follow the guidelines in this book you will avoid any problems.

Q *How should cortisone creams be applied?*
A See Appendix 1. Briefly, however, the following guidelines apply: use as much or as little as is needed to cover the area in question when rubbed in well. Do not dab tentatively at the rash and then wipe away almost the whole lot with a tissue! The cream will promote healing from deeper layers of the skin so rub it in well, but use only as much as is needed to cover the rash. Do not use thick layers of cream to promote a quicker healing process.

Q *What are the side-effects of cortisone creams?*
A See Appendix 1.

Q *Is eczema due to a nervous disorder?*
A No. Eczema is a distinct disease of the skin (see Chapter 2) and is not brought on by tension, stress or anxiety. However, there is no doubt that during periods of stress your child will rub more at areas of unhealed skin. Your best approach to such events is to go for total skin control so that your child can have the full range of emotions, from joy to sorrow, without scratching.

Q *Is homoeopathy or hypnosis useful in eczema or psoriasis?*
A Anything that is safe and exerts any positive influence on chronic skin conditions is fine by most doctors. However, my own feeling is that the correct use of the medications prescribed in orthodox medicine is of much more importance in these conditions. In particular, I feel that such procedures only deflect attention away from the correct approach towards resolving these skin problems.

Q *Does acupuncture help any skin disorders?*
A No. Unfortunately acupuncture does not seem to improve the lot of anyone suffering from chronic skin conditions.

Q *Do any detergents irritate childrens' skin?*
A Yes. Some children with sensitive skin will start to itch and scratch if certain washing powder residues come next to their skin. The main offenders are those promoted by the manufacturers as *biological* and containing *enzymes*.

If you have suspicions that your washing powder is causing problems then try and rid your machine of all traces of the powder as follows: clean out the soap tray thoroughly and run the machine through a hot wash programme, with no powder and no clothes. In dramatic cases it may be advisable to rinse out all clean clothes, linens and towels as well to get rid of any traces of the offending powder from these fabrics.

The safest detergents for machine washing are the low-lather type and the supermarkets' 'own brands' are often excellent. You must not, however, confuse *low-lather* with *low-temperature* powders, as these *do* contain unsuitable enzymes.

Q *Do any soaps or cosmetics cause skin problems?*
A Yes. If your child has any skin condition or just dry sensitive skin always choose a simple, *non-scented* soap. For very sensitive skins use a soap substitute such as Emollient Oilatum. Your chemist will give advice on the correct products.

Many cosmetics can aggravate pre-existing skin problems or even cause skin eruptions. Teenagers with acne tend to overcompensate with thick layers of camouflaging make-up and these often cause problems. Try and remember that all skin healing requires cleanliness and plenty of air – so encourage thorough cleaning and less make-up. If any cosmetics are to be used then go for the Almay brand of hypo-allergenic products.

Q *Should all moles be left alone?*

A Certainly they should not be picked at or rubbed but treated like any other area of skin. However, if you find your child picking or rubbing at a particular mole then have your doctor look at it in case there are reasons to have it removed.

Q *Are all warts contagious?*

A Most are, and they seem to spread by personal contact or from picking at one wart, making it bleed, and rubbing the blood onto adjacent skin. Better to treat any wart eruption quickly and effectively (see Chapter 2 and Appendix 3) so that no further transmission can occur.

Q *Is acne due to dirt?*

A No. The causes of acne are described in Chapter 2.

Q *Are herpes skin infections the same as sexually transmitted herpes?*

A No. The three types of herpes mentioned in Chapter 2 have nothing to do with sexual contact.

Q *If my child has school sores (impetigo) should he/she be kept from school or friends?*

A Yes. This is a particularly infectious type of skin condition and will spread very quickly. You should keep your child out of circulation until you are sure the infection has cleared.

Q *Are ointments better than creams for skin problems?*

A Whether an ointment or a cream is used depends to a certain extent on the condition being treated. Where there is a choice, children and their parents tend to prefer creams, as they disappear quickly when rubbed in and they don't stick to the child's clothes as much as ointments. However, ointments work better as a treatment as they deliver the medicine they contain more effectively than creams.

Q *Should I use dusting powders on my baby?*

A My own feeling is that too many babies are given too liberal a coating of dusting powders for no good reason other than tradition. Think logically about it yourself – do you powder your bottom every day? There is a feeling that dusting powders are useful while babies are in nappies but I have my doubts about any effect. Certainly when there is any suggestion of nappy rash putting a layer of powder onto the inflamed skin only prevents a natural healing process by blocking the pores and preventing air circulation. It is advisable to clear a 'caked' bottom of damp powder and allow a few hours out of nappies. This promotes better healing.

When your baby is in nappies and has healthy skin, leave well alone and perhaps only use a barrier preparation which will keep urine and faeces away from the skin. Powder will 'cake' when wet and actually makes the area moist and prone to inflammation.

Appendix 1

Cortisone Skin Preparations

Cortisone is a hormone produced in all of us which can be artifically manufactured. It has an *anti-inflammatory* effect, and for this reason is widely used in the treatment of skin conditions. It is used in tablet, injection, inhaler, cream and ointment form for such conditions as *asthma*, *eczema* and *hay-fever*, and is also called *topical steroid* or just *steroid*.

Here we will be concerned with the creams and ointments applied directly onto diseased or damaged skin. Many different brands are available, containing different types of steroid and in different strengths, which we shall call *very strong*, *strong*, *moderate*, *weak* and *very weak*. A list of brands available in Britain and Ireland is given in the table below, along with the chemical name of the cortisone it contains. Some of these also contain an antibiotic (these have an *A*, *C* or *N* after the brand name) and others are combination skin preparations where the cortisone is one of two or more active ingredients (these are marked with an asterisk).

If you are prescribed a cortisone treatment it is very important that you follow your doctor's instructions to the letter. These drugs are completely safe when used correctly – only if you disregard your doctor's advice are you likely to experience any side-effects. Bear in mind that any decision you make to ignore your doctor's advice will be reflected in the final appearance of your child's skin. If he/she has prescribed a cortisone treatment, *use it* – more skin damage is caused by withholding treatment than could possibly come about *even* from using it incorrectly.

Those treatments in the *weak* or *very weak* categories are the safest preparations and can be used for long periods without side-effects. Those in the *moderate* category may be used for reasonably long periods (say up to a month) without side-effects. However they should *not* be used on the face *except* in short, sharp treatments – of no longer than one day's therapy. Those in the *strong* and *very strong* categories should be used until healing occurs and then discontinued. A special 'weaning' plan is useful when using these preparations (see below for details). They should not be used for long periods as side-effects will occur. They should *not* be used on the face.

The amount of cream or ointment to use depends on the extent and severity of the rash; how long it has been present; any complicating

Trade name	Generic name
Very strong	
Dermovate	clobetasol 0.5%
Halciderm	halcinonide 0.1%
Strong	
Diprosone, Diprosalic	
*Betnovate-C, *Betnovate-N	betamethasone
*Fucibet	
Topisolon	desoxymethasone
Nerisone, Temetex	diflucortolone
Topilar	fluclorolone
*Synalar-C	fluocinolone acetonide
*Synalar-N	
Metosyn	fluocinonide
*Locoid-C	hydrocortisone butyrate
Remiderm	triamcinolone
Aristocort, Aureocort	
Kenacomb, Kenacort	
Ledercort	
Moderate	
Betnovate R.D.	betamethasone
Eumovate	clobetasone butyrate 0.05%
Ultradil, Ultralanum	fluocortolone
*Haelan-C	fluocortolone
Weak	
*Alphaderm	hydrocortisone 1%,
*Calmurid HC	with urea
Modrasone	alclometasone
Hydrocortisyl	hydrocortisone 1%
*Eczederm	hydrocortisone 1%
*Vioform-Hydrocortisone	hydrocortisone 1%
Very weak	
*Alphosyl HC	hydrocortisone 0.5%
Dioderm	hydrocortisone 0.1%
Dome-Cort	hydrocortisone 0.125%
*Eurax-Hydrocortisone	hydrocortisone 0.25%
*Combination treatments	

factors, (such as infection); and the underlying cause. Apply enough to cover the affected area and rub it in well. You'll be surprised at how little is actually needed to cover what seems like a large area. Remember that the cream or ointment is being used to reduce inflammation and promote healing. If you only dab the cream or ointment on and then wipe almost the whole lot away you are unlikely to get any improvement at all.

A treatment programme

Quite often parents notice a dramatic improvement in their child's skin (particularly in *atopic eczema*) when one of the stronger preparations is used. However, the delight turns to dismay quite soon after the cream or ointment is stopped as the rash reappears and looks as bad as before. We now recognize that the skin needs to be 'weaned' off the strong creams gradually in a step-by-step procedure, so that eventually only a very mild cream (or even just a moisturizer) is needed to keep the skin healthy.

Let us suppose that a *very strong* cortisone has been prescribed for your child's skin complaint. If you use it until the complaint clears completely and then simply stop the treatment, the rash may well return. What you must do instead is switch instead to a *strong* treatment, then a *moderate* one, and so on until you are just using a *moisturizer*. A typical treatment is illustrated in the diagram overleaf, where one drug has been selected at each strength as an example, beginning with a very strong one as step 1. Your doctor may start the child off with a lower-strength drug, that is on a lower rung of the ladder, in which case the complaint must be cleared up with the *first* preparation used before going down onto the next rung.

Each step can be extended or shortened depending on the speed of recovery and how long the rash was present before treatment was started – except of course the first stage of treatment. Do *not* be tempted to skip stages, otherwise a breakthrough reaction could occur. If you're following this procedure as described and the complaint flares up again as you move down the ladder, go back up a step and stay at that level for a few extra days – you can then try a lower strength again and will probably find that the skin will remain clear. In some severe cases of *eczema* you might find it difficult to go below step 4 of the treatment ladder – however, step 4 (weak) preparations can be used for a long time without problems.

Step 1: Dermovate.
Apply twice daily to all affected areas until the skin has completely healed and then for three more days.

Step 2: Betnovate.
Apply twice daily to the same previously affected areas for three days.

Step 3: Eumovate.
Apply twice daily to the same areas for three days.
Step 4: Hydrocortisyl.
Apply twice daily to the same area for five days.

Step 5: Dioderm.
Apply twice daily to the same areas for ten days.

Step 6: Moisturizer.
Three to five times daily for 14 days. Apply liberally.

A typical treatment programme using cortisone preparations.

Even if you achieve a total clearance and all is going well, bear in mind you might get an outbreak of inflammation some time in the future. If so, nip any inflamed area in the bud by choosing one rung of the ladder as a treatment and applying that cream or ointment until control is achieved again. However always work back down the ladder from rungs 1, 2, or 3. You will find that you can shorten the treatment times considerably with an aggressive early intervention and also use less and less cream or ointment for each outbreak. In addition the outbreaks should become less and less frequent as time progresses.

If one or two areas seem resistant to healing compared with others then continue to work down the ladder on the healed areas. In *atopic eczema* hands, wrists and ankles are often slower to heal, and need longer treatment with stronger preparations.

The face must be treated differently. Only use preparations from step 3 downwards. Step 3 can only be used for one to two days' therapy and then a reduction to step 4 must occur. However steps 4 and 5 can be used more frequently and liberally to heal the skin. Otherwise the same basic principles apply: go for total control and don't jump the stages.

Other than on the face, the use of *strong* and *very strong* creams or ointments is entirely justified to heal the skin and no side-effects will be experienced in the time-spans over which this programme is used. If the programme seems not to be working at all then the diagnosis is almost certainly incorrect.

Side-effects

First of all, remember that, used sensibly, logically and correctly, cortisone preparations will cause *no* side-effects. Secondly, remember that *weak* and *very weak* preparations can be used for long periods without side-effects. Thirdly, remember that *strong* and *very strong* preparations should not be used on the face, and the *moderate* preparations should not be used on the face for more than two days. Finally, remember that *moderate*, *strong* and *very strong* preparations should not be used for long-term treatment.

On the skin itself the main reactions, if too much of a *strong* topical steroid is used for too long, are stretching and thinning of the skin and possibly increased growth of hair. The stretching shows itself rather in the way a woman gets stretch marks on her tummy after pregnancy, with creases on the skin and a loss of elasticity. The thinning will reveal blood vessels through the skin, and particularly in the face this may lead to a rather ruddy complexion. Bruising of the skin may occur after very minor surgery. It may also mean more damage done by scratching and slower healing of cuts and cracks. If caught in time, such reactions are mostly reversible and a weaker hydrocortisone or plain cream used for a period will improve the skin condition. But one word of warning – never panic and stop a strong steroid overnight after long-term use. This can lead to a rebound reaction so that the rash temporarily becomes worse than ever. Instead gradually wean the skin on to something weaker, perhaps over a week or two or even longer.

The other side-effects are internal bodily reactions, and since a great deal of steroid has to be absorbed into the blood stream for these to take place they are unlikely to result from the correct use of topical steroids. These internal reactions include a swelling of the face ('moonface' as it is called); the slowing up of growth in babies and children; and adrenal suppression. This last means the artificial steroids might lessen the production of natural hydrocortisone by the body so that if your child has an infection or shock there is less resistance. It is also possible to develop eye problems.

Such side-effects, if they develop at all, are almost always as a result of using the stronger preparations over most of the skin surface (particularly in babies). Nevertheless, they are a very good reason for using topical treatment with care and wisdom.

So there you have it! Cortisone skin preparations are among the most widely prescribed (and safest) treatments available. Do make sure you know and understand their correct use.

Appendix 2

Treating Skin Infections

Your child's skin can be infected by bacteria, viruses, fungi and yeasts. I will now list the commonly prescribed treatments for these individual 'bugs'. Bear in mind one simple but important basic principle in these treatments: if the infection is fairly small and localized then some form of topical preparation (to be applied directly onto the skin) is likely to be prescribed – usually as a cream; however, for stubborn or widespread infections tablets may be suggested in addition to the local cream to promote a speedier clearance.

Treatments used against viruses

Three preparations are commonly used:

- *Herplex-D* (idoxuridine 0.1%). This comes as a 10ml solution and should be applied hourly during the day and given a liberal application last thing at night.
- *Zostrum* (idoxuridine 5%). This comes as a 5ml solution and should be applied four times daily for four days, commencing treatment as soon as possible (as soon as the rash is seen to erupt).
- *Zovirax* (acylovir). This comes as a cream and tablets. The cream is applied five times daily at four-hourly intervals for five days. The tablets are only occasionally used – mainly for shingles.

Treatments used against bacteria

There is an extremely long list of antibiotic creams and ointments for use in skin disorders and it might confuse to list all of them. However I have set out below the most commonly prescribed with their trade name first and generic (chemical) name in brackets. Remember that antibiotic tablets are also used in resistant or large areas of skin infection. Most of the following preparations come as creams and ointments. Their application is very much dependent on the type of infection but around four times daily is normal. Do remember to wash your hands carefully after applying any preparation to infected skin, otherwise you may carry the infection and spread it elsewhere (including to yourself). In addition, I suggest your child has his/her own towels for use during any infection and that these are put in a hot wash after the infection has cleared.

- Achromycin (tetracycline) ointment
- Aureomycin (chlortetracyline) cream and ointment
- Bactroban (mupirocin) ointment
- Betadine (povidone-iodine) lotion, spray, gauze, sachets
- Cetavlex (cetrimide) cream
- Cicatrin (neomycin) cream and powder
- Flamazine (silver sulphadiazine) cream
- Framygen (framycetin sulphate) cream
- Fucidin (sodium fusidate) gel, cream, ointment
- Genticin (gentamycin sulphate) cream, ointment
- Soframycin (framycetin sulphate) cream, ointment

There is, of course, an equally wide range of oral antibiotics.

Treatments used against fungi and yeasts

There is a wide range of anti-fungal skin preparations and I have listed the most frequently prescribed below. Where you see an *H* after the name it means that a mild hydrocortisone is added to promote a speedier healing of the skin and reduce the itch associated with fungal or yeast infections. The preparations are listed as trade name with the generic (chemical name) in brackets.

- Batrafen (ciclopiroxolamine) cream, powder, solution
- Canesten (clotrimazole) cream and solution
- Daktarin (H) (miconazole nitrate) cream, powder
- Ecostatin (econazole nitrate) cream
- Exelderm (sulconazole nitrate) cream
- Mycostatin (nystatin) ointment and powder
- Nystaform (nystatin) cream, ointment
- Pimafucin (natamycin) cream
- Tinaderm (tolnaftate) cream, solution, powder
- Travogyn (isoconazole nitrate) cream and solution

These are usually prescribed for use three or four times daily. The preparation should be rubbed in well.

For resistant or widespread fungal or yeast infections the following oral preparations are used:

- Daktarin (miconazole) tablets and injection
- Fulcin (griseofulvin) tablets and oral suspension

- Fungilin (amphotericin) tablet
- Grisovin (griseofulvin) tablet
- Mycostatin (nystatin) tablet and oral suspension
- Nizoral (ketoconazole) tablet
- Pimafucin (natamycin) tablet and oral suspension

Because of potential side-effects (nausea, irritability, liver damage) associated with some oral preparations they are usually reserved for severe infections. An exception is Mycostatin – often used as a suspension for children.

Treatments used against acne

The mainstay of treatment in most cases of acne are antibiotics. These are usually prescribed for a minimum of three months and *must* be taken as directed. There are three main groups:

- tetracyclines
- Minocin (minocycline)
- Vibramycin (doxycline)

Tetracyclines, usually prescribed in dosages of 250 mg to be taken four times daily, *must* be taken on an empty stomach, that is to say, at least an hour before meals, and *never* with milk or antacids. The other two can be taken with food or milk, and the usual dosage is 50 mg twice daily.

Where there is a suspicion that the acne 'bugs' are resistant to these antibiotics then either erythromycin (250 mg four times daily) or co-trimoxazole (twice or three times daily) is often prescribed.

In some girls with acne a hormonal approach is used with a preparation called Diane (cyproterone). Treatment involves a 28-day cycle, with the preparation taken once daily for 21 days, followed be a week's break. This preparation also has a contraceptive effect.

Appendix 3

Cryotherapy

Cryotherapy is a treatment routine used in certain skin disorders. It has been used in the United States for some 20 years, but has only recently been introduced in other countries. It involves the use of intense cold (down to −200°C) to destroy unwanted skin blemishes. The tissue to be removed is frozen as described below and the final result is almost always cosmetically very acceptable. A number of different machines are used, all of which work on the same principle, so I shall describe only the one I use.

The machine I use is called a Cryo-Surg unit and looks like a thermos flask with a special 'gun' attachment at the top. Various sizes of brass probes (small brass instruments of differing diameters at the tip) can be connected to the gun head. Liquid nitrogen is put into the thermos body and the gun attachment is screwed on tightly. A trigger is then pressed and the liquid nitrogen is pumped up and through the brass probe, escaping via an exhaust.

As the gas passes through the probe it is frozen to −200°C. If the probe is placed against diseased skin it sticks and freezes the area as deeply and as wide as required. At very low temperatures the tissue cells die and the area is effectively destroyed. Nature sets up an immediate separation process to peel away the frozen tissue and produce healing at the junction of the frozen and normal tissue. The end result is cosmetically very acceptable and almost scar-free.

Cryotherapy (known also as *cryosurgery*) is used to treat a wide variety of skin blemishes, including *warts*, *moles*, *verrucae*, *molluscum contagiosum*, skin lumps, skin *cancers* and some *cysts*. It is also used extensively in other surgical treatments. The beauty of cryotherapy is that no cutting, burning or other destructive techniques are used so that there is no bleeding, relatively little discomfort, no need for hospitalization, and a very acceptable and speedy result. For details of a doctor near you who uses cryotherapy, contact:

Dr Philip Hopkins,
249 Haverstock Hill,
London NW3 4PS
Tel: 01-749 3759

Dr Paul Carson,
70 St Laurence's Park,
Stillorgan,
Co. Dublin
Tel: 01-831143

The Role of Diet and Food Additives

In some of the long-standing or recurring skin problems of children a close look at diet may give clues as to the underlying cause or possible aggravating factors. Altering the diet to avoid suspected harmful foods can make all the difference for children with certain conditions.

The role of diet in children's skin disorders is often controversial, with some doctors keen enthusiasts and others total sceptics. The truth probably lies somewhere in between, that only a small but well-defined group of skin problems are improved by dietary manipulation.

The underlying theory of the connection between diet and the skin disorders listed below is that your child may be allergic to certain foods, or additives within the foods. If one of these products is eaten or drunk a reaction occurs in the stomach and intestines with the release of certain chemicals, which doctors call hormones. These chemicals circulate in the bloodstream and produce (or aggravate) certain skin conditions. For example, urticaria is often an allergic response on the skin to certain foodstuffs. The initial allergic reaction occurs in the stomach or intestines, but the end result appears on the skin.

While certain foods, such as dairy products or eggs, can cause skin problems in their usual consumed form, other foods would be perfectly safe were it not for the chemicals which are added to them. Nowadays many additives are used to make the final produce more commercially attractive to the buyer. For example, packaged bacon looks the way it does by the use of a colouring agent. Without this additive it would look as if the bacon had 'gone off'. Similarly, some orange squashes look nice and 'orangey' because they contain a colouring agent. In this way products are made to appeal to the eye and look good to eat or drink.

Unfortunately, the use of artificial chemicals in food processing has caused health problems as some people, especially children, are very sensitive to these compounds and react in different ways. The reaction can be in the form of overactive behaviour, a worsening of eczema or an episode of wheezing.

The individual chemicals have very long names so that a coding system has been devised to identify them individually. Each chemical has a specific number with a capital E in front. For example, E102 is tartrazine, a yellow colouring agent; E123 is amaranth, a red colouring agent. The various additives have different functions such as colouring, flavouring or preserving foodstuffs. Quite often one product may contain many different additives, for flavouring, colouring and preserving. In the diets below the individual additives to be avoided are listed by their 'E number', which appears on the label. If you think one of them is causing your child's problem, check everything you buy carefully.

Here is a list of the conditions where a close look at your child's diet may prove very useful in achieving control without relying so much on medication.

Condition	*Diet*
Atopic eczema – mild	a or b
– moderate	a, b, c
– severe	a, b, c, d (also g or h in certain cases)
Atopic eczema associated with asthma and nasal polyps (see Appendix 7)	e and f highly recommended
Mouth ulcers	a, e, f, g
Urticaria/angio-oedema	e and f

Key to diets

Avoid
(a) Milk
(b) Milk and egg
(c) Milk, egg, colourings and preservatives
(d) Milk, egg, nuts, tomatoes, fish, colourings and preservatives
(e) Azo-dyes and benzoates (see details below)
(f) Salicylates
(g) Gluten
(h) All wheat

The diets

(a) *Milk-free* Avoid milk, cream, cheese, chocolate, yoghurt, butter, ice-cream, ordinary margarine, products containing *casein* and *whey* (milk proteins), milk puddings such as custards, creamed rice, baby cereals fortified with milk solids, Ovaltine and similar milky drinks, tinned or packed soup labelled 'Cream of . . . .'

(b) *Milk/egg-free* As above, plus eggs in pure form (scrambled, poached etc.) or in baking (meringues, quiches, pavlovas etc.), tinned or processed foods containing egg.

(c) *Milk/egg colouring and preservative-free* As for a and b above with special attention paid to avoiding all processed foods containing the following food additives: E102 (tartrazine), E104 (quinoline yellow), E107 (yellow 2G), E110 (sunset yellow FCF), E122 (azorubine), E123 (amaranth), E124 (ponceau 4R or cochineal Red A), E127 (erythrosine), E220–227 inclusive (sulphur dioxide and sulphites), E249–251 inclusive (nitrites and nitrates), E320 (butylated hydroxyanisole), E321 (butylated hydroxytoluene), E621–623 (the glutamates, e.g. monosodium glutamate).

These are likely to be found in syrups and vitamin medicines, coloured sweets and tablets (especially orange, red, green, yellow), and coloured toothpastes. Check every food package before buying any item. Watch out especially for supermarket packaged meats, fish fingers, canned meats and fish, flavoured milks, coloured cheeses, packaged soups, flavoured foods, flavoured crisps, fruit squashes and fizzy drinks, lozenges and cough syrups, most confectionery, sauces, pickles and jams, unless home-made. Use only white toothpaste.

(d) *Milk/egg/nuts/tomatoes/fish/colouring and preservative-free* As diet c plus the elimination of nuts, tomatoes and fish. This includes tomato ketchup and flavourings, fish pastes and all forms of nuts and nut oils.

(e) *Azo-dye and benzoic acid-free* This is a specific group of food additives as listed below which are notorious offenders in some allergic conditions. Because their chemical structure is so similar to salicylates this type of diet is usually combined with a salicylate-free approach (diet f).

Avoid E102 (tartrazine), E104 (quinoline yellow), E107 (yellow 2G), E110 (sunset yellow 2F), E122 (azorubine), E123 (amaranth), E124 (ponceau 4R), E127 (erythrosine), E128 (red 2G), E131 (patent blue) E132 (indigo carmine), E210–219 inclusive (benzoic acid and benzoates).

(f) *Salicylate-free* The common medicine aspirin has the potential to trigger reactions in susceptible individuals. A form of aspirin occurs naturally in some foods and so aspirin-sensitive people must avoid these as well. Aspirin is often found in cough medicines and decongestants where it may be labelled in the original chemical name of acetyl salicylic acid (or just salicylate). In addition the chemical structure of aspirin is so similar to the Azo-dyes and benzoates (see diet e) that any diet involving the elimination of aspirin will almost always be combined with the elimination of those food additives listed in e above.

Avoid aspirin, disprin or any medicine containing acetyl salicylic acid or salicylate. In addition avoid the following foods which contain naturally occurring aspirin: dried fruits, berry fruits, oranges, apricots, pineapples, cucumbers, gherkins, tomato sauce, tea, endive, olives, grapes, almonds, liquorice, peppermints, honey, Worcester sauce.

(g) *Gluten-free* When we eat wheat in any form, such as in bread, biscuits, cakes or pastries, it contains a protein called gluten. Some children and adults are sensitive to the gluten component of wheat and develop a condition of the bowel called coeliac disease. However, an unusual variant of gluten sensitivity occurs in some highly allergic individuals, who have the combination problem of asthma, eczema, nasal polyps (fleshy growths found inside the nose) and vague abdominal pains. In particular their asthma and eczema tend to be difficult to control. If you have a child with severe eczema, especially if he/she has other associated allergies, then a three month trial of gluten-free wheat may be suggested by your doctor.

On this diet check carefully that the food does not contain gluten, flour (unless gluten-free), wheat flour, wheat starch, wheat protein, wheat germ, or edible starch. Examples of food likely to contain gluten include: bread, crisp-breads, popadums, chapatis, breakfast cereals, chocolate and other sweets, cornflour, biscuits, cakes, pastries, puddings, deserts, meat or fish in breadcrumbs or sauce or batter, sausages, gravies, sauces, soups, stock cubes, soy sauce, pasta, semolina, processed cheeses, cheese spreads and communion wafers.

A booklet, *Gluten-Free Manufactured Food Lists* may be obtained from your local Coeliac Society. This is a self-help group of coeliac disease patients who offer help and advice on the condition and the associated diets. There are Coeliac Societies in almost every province throughout Britain and Ireland and your local telephone directory will have the address and number of a branch near you.

Some gluten-free products such as biscuits, flour and pasta are available from your chemist on a National Health Service prescription. Check with your local pharmacist for details. When baking with gluten-free flour it is better to make a small loaf or rolls rather than a large loaf. Bread should be mixed to a batter rather than a dough.

(h) *Wheat-free* This is a much more dramatic and restrictive diet than the gluten-free one. It may be tried with diet c in an attempt to clear up any severe eczema where allergies such as asthma are present.

On a wheat-free diet look for the wheat-free symbol – a **W** in bold type – on manufactured foods. A list of foods containing wheat is set out in diet g. Check carefully that the food does not contain gluten, flour, wheat flour, wheat starch, wheat protein, wheatgerm or edible starch. Instead of wheat use flours made from arrowroot, millet, buck wheat, rice, soya, potato, peas and chickpeas. Rice does not contain any wheat and is a useful standby.

Important

When considering these diets please remember that only some conditions respond to dietary manipulation. You must involve your family doctor and local dietitian before subjecting your child to any diet. Any diet should be given at least a six week trial before deciding that it has or has not worked. If there is no improvement, accept that this is so and do not go chasing other fad diets.

Remember also that some diets are antisocial and demanding for children. Do not create a separate problem while trying to solve a minor one.

Hints and Tips on Clothes

If you have a child with a long-standing skin condition such as eczema, or even just a toddler with dry, sensitive skin then clothing can be important in keeping the child comfortable. Some fabrics irritate while others are more suitable close to the skin. If you pay attention to the detail of the clothes you choose it can often make the difference between an overheated, itchy, irritable child and a more tranquil, less sensitive, comfortable child.

Have a read at the guidelines in this section and try and put the advice into practice. There are addresses for all materials throughout the text.

Basic Principles

The most important factors when choosing clothes for your child are that they should not irritate the skin and they must prevent the child from scratching. Even tiny children can be very ingenious in order to reach an itch, but they must be stopped at all costs. Your child's clothes should, as far as possible, be made of cotton fabric or yarn, and be loosely fitting but scratchproof. Cotton allows the skin to breathe, it is absorbent and isn't harsh on a sensitive skin. Wool is too hot and too harsh, while synthetics do not allow the skin to breathe, and cause over-heating. Polyester/cotton mixtures may be all right as long as the proportion of cotton is fairly high. Acrylic can also be a useful standby, as long as the garment is losely woven or knitted, and feels soft. Remember, too, that some cotton fabrics may not be suitable. For example, thick denim is hard and hot on a warm day, and 'T-shirt' fabric may be too warm in summer even if it is 100% cotton.

The most practical style for daywear for small children is dungarees and a cotton shirt with cuffs, or an all-in-one suit with cuffs. Nightwear is also a problem. Stretch-suits, even if they are mostly cotton, can be too hot because they are close fitting. You could, of course, buy the brushed cotton pyjamas available from Adams or Mothercare, but remember that the elasticated sleeves may cause irritation, and a baby can easily get under this type of pyjama and have a good scratch!

If you have a baby or small toddler with atopic eczema he may need to wear mittens to prevent the little fingers from scratching and damaging the inflamed skin. Cotton mittens can be bought from Mothercare or Adams Childrenswear, or you can make them yourself from cotton scraps. If your baby has eczema of the scalp then a cotton bonnet will lessen the damage done by scratching and also hide the affected area. A simple bonnet can be easily stitched together from bits of cotton leftovers.

It is possible to buy 100% cotton garments and best value here are dungarees, but beware of clothes that are a bit skimpy and leave too much flesh exposed to scratching fingers. Check the elastic and make sure it is strong and covered in cotton – exposed rubber will irritate the skin.

Most babywear shops and departments have some cotton underwear and cotton dungarees. Clothkits – 24 High Street, Lewes, Sussex BN7 2LU – have some very practical lightweight cotton dungarees, many in kit form for you to make up.

Specializing in garments less readily available in cotton are two mail order firms:

- Bidelen, 81 Park Road, Sale, Cheshire, M33 1JA, is a Swedish firm with a range of knitted cotton jumpers, playsuits, bonnets, mittens, etc.
- Cotton On, Bandside House, Great Plumpton, Kirkham, Lancs, was started by a mother of an eczematous child can supply stocking socks, tights, pyjamas and underwear for tinies, and jumpers for children of two and over. In addition, the National Eczema Society can supply cotton knee-length socks in size 6 upwards.

Outdoor Wear

Many children – especially those with eczema – have a good internal 'central heating' and can be easily overheated with the wrong clothing. Indeed children with eczema can quite often tolerate cold weather with seemingly less clothes than would appear adequate. Dress for the child's comfort, not your worries about what the neighbours think! Use lots of layers of cotton rather than one layer of wool close to the skin, and moisturize liberally all the child's exposed skin, especially in windy weather.

If it is wet you may have to put your toddler in a splash-suit, but prevent contact with the skin wherever possible and do not leave it on any longer than necessary – a slight damping may be better for the child than the over-heating caused by the nylon of the suit!

In summer months your child will probably be more comfortable in a light cardigan over one layer of cotton, and if it really gets hot keep him in the shade for reasonable periods of time to prevent overheating.

As autumn approaches a cotton anorak (home-made in cotton jersey or similar) is ideal, and colder days are best met with a suit in cotton quilting – double-sided quilting makes the job easier! The acrylic suits which you can buy ready made may be useful, although elasticated wrists and ankles could cause trouble.

If you wish to knit or make your own clothes for your child then the following points may help: knitting materials should be soft, smooth acrylic or, better still, cotton yarn. Another alternative is to use an acrylic/nylon/wool mixture to make tank tops, as these do not come in contact with the skin, and are loose fitting, and so less likely to cause overheating.

By far the best fastener is the button, because it is less easily undone by little fingers than poppers or Velcro. The latter can be useful, however, on all-in-one pyjama legs to allow opening for nappy changing. (Remember to do the Velcro up before washing or it will stick to all the other garments). Zips are, of course, ideal in jumpsuits and anoraks, and neither metal nor nylon zips cause any extra irritation.

It should be noted that trousers which button onto tops are not a good idea. The eczematic wriggles so much in his attempts to scratch that the buttons will quickly be ripped off. On the same principle loose-weave fabrics are a waste of money, as they will quickly be ripped when your child does his strange contortions to reach that itch. Buttonholes should be firmly stitched and only fractionally larger than the button, otherwise the button-hole will stretch, and your child will be scratching away again! In order to beat night-time scratching use pyjamas with a collarless, back-fastening top and bottom in dungaree style with built in feet.

Bedclothes

You will be amazed at how hot your child can get in bed, and for someone who has eczema heat equals itchiness, scratching and lack of sleep. Put away all your cot blankets unless they are very light cotton, or possibly thin acrylic. Then invest in a rubber sheet (from chemists) to put on top of the plastic mattress, as plastic can also cause over-heating. Next see that the sheets are cotton, or at least cotton/polyester. Flanellette sheets may be too warm in summer, but can be used instead of blankets. In hot weather your baby will need no covers at all. In winter a terylene-filled quilt is the best answer because it is light and does not press on the skin as blankets do. Alternatively, buy some cotton cellular blankets, which you can get from Limericks, 100 Hamlet Court Road, Westcliff-on-sea, Essex, or Celaric Ltd., Willows Mill, Lepton, Huddersfield.

HINTS AND TIPS ON CLOTHES

The information for this section was obtained from the National Eczema Society who have a wide range of excellent, practical pamphlets dealing with skin care etc., for children with eczema and sensitive skin.

Appendix 6

How to Identify That Skin Problem

In the average child's lifetime he or she will develop numerous lumps, bumps, rashes and eruptions on the skin. The majority will come and go in days without the need for medical attention and quite often will be identified by neighbours, grandparents etc. who have seen it all before. Some rashes are like identifying elephants – once seen, never mistaken again! An example of this is chicken pox with its very definite blisters, widespread distribution and marked itch. However, grannies, uncles and the know-all next door aren't foolproof, so I have drawn up guidelines to help you pin point the exact name of your child's rash or blemish. Once you have the name you can refer to the main text in this book for details of causes, complications and treatments.

There are important questions you can ask yourself at the beginning of the search, the answers to which should guide you to the correct sections and a firm diagnosis. While there may appear to be a great deal of overlap in these lists, by cross referring from one to another you will soon narrow it down to one or two possibilities.

Even if you can't tell definitely what the problem is, there are other questions here which will help you help your doctor with his/her diagnosis. I've also included a list of the most common skin problems, so you can see what it's *likely* to be. However, please remember that the following can only be general guidelines; they are not carved in stone and will not cover every variation on the same theme.

First of all, ask yourself these questions:

1)   Where is the rash/eruption/blemish and where did it start?

You should notice where the rash started and if it spread quickly, as both can be useful for diagnosis.

Widespread	*Face*	*Central trunk only*
eczema	impetigo	pityriasis versicolor
scabies	eczema	pityriasis rosea
psoriasis	psoriasis	herpes zoster
urticaria	herpes simplex	virus rash
drug reaction	acne	
	virus	

Mainly hands/feet	Creases of elbow/knee	Mouth
eczema	eczema	ulcers
fungus	psoriasis	herpes simplex
psoriasis	seborrhoeic eczema	candida
warts	fungus	measles
insect bites	candida	
	pediculosis	Nails
Scalp		psoriasis
psoriasis		fungus
seborrhoiec eczema		eczema
pediculosis		
fungus		Penis
chicken-pox		scabies

2) *Did the rash/eruption/blemish appear quickly or did the child only gradually become aware of it?*

The more suddenly it appears the sooner it's likely to need attention.

Very suddenly – over hours or days	Over a few days or a week	Present for weeks or months
urticaria	eczema	psoriasis
eczema (especially contact eczema)	impetigo	eczema
	scabies	fungus
insect bites	pediculosis	warts
drug reaction	drug reaction	
herpes	pityriasis rosea	
virus rash	psoriasis	
	fungus	
	candida	

3) *Is the rash itchy?*

Very	Moderately	Often not
urticaria	fungus	warts
eczema	psoriasis	fungus
scabies	drug reaction	impetigo
pediculosis	pityriasis rosea	psoriasis
insect bites	candida	drug reaction
drug reaction		

101

- *Does anything make it better or worse?*
  For example urticaria can be aggravated by certain foods or food additives; equally the itch of tinea pedis is eased by keeping feet bare.
- *Has the child been in contact with anyone with a similar problem?*
  This is important in such contagious problems as measles, chicken pox etc. and will give an important clue to diagnosis in unusual or mild variants of these conditions.
- *Is your child on any medication or using any cream?*
  This is important in puzzling rashes where the cause may be due to a reaction to certain medicines such as antibiotics.

Now that you have answered these questions, look at the list immediately below which sets out the most frequently encountered skin problems in children. Remember that one of these is the most likely explantion for your child's skin problem.

Infections
        viral   – warts
                                   herpes simplex/zoster
                                   general rash due to virus
        bacterial – fungal – impetigo tinea
                                   candida
Acne
Psoriasis
Eczema
Urticaria – acute and chronic
         – papular – pediculosis
                       scabies
                       insect bites
Drug reactions

Glossary of medical terms

Words in **bold type** are defined or explained further elsewhere in the glossary or in chapter 2.

Acclaim Spray used to get rid of **house dust mites.**

allergen Any substance capable of producing an **allergic reaction** – for example, grass pollen is a hay-fever allergen.

allergic reaction An abnormal response to a substance tolerated well by normal (non-allergic) individuals (see also **allergen**).

allergy Tissue sensitivity to certain substances – **asthma, eczema** and hay fever are all conditions due to allergy.

antibiotics Medicines used to treat infections due to **bacteria.**

antihistamine A type of drug used to block the effect of histamine, a **hormone** released in many **allergic reactions** which produces many different symptoms, such as itching.

artificial colours and preservatives Chemicals added during food processing to extend the shelf life, or make more colourful, or enhance the taste and appearance of various packaged foods.

Artilin – 3A A paint which kills **house dust mites** on contact.

asthma The label used to describe the collection of symptoms of coughing, wheezing and shortness of breath.

bacterium (pl. *bacteria*) The name given to the 'bugs' which cause such infections as bronchitis and **cellulitis.**

beclomethasone Chemical name for a group of **cortisone** drugs.

Beconase **Cortisone** spray for use in nasal allergies.

Betnesol **Cortisone**-based drops for use in eye, nose and ear conditions.

benign In medical parlance this is used to describe a non-cancerous condition.

benzoate Name given to a group of food additives.

benzoyl peroxide A specific anti-acne skin preparation.

benzyl benzoate A lotion for treating **scabies.**

capillaries The smallest of all blood vessels.

cetrimide An antiseptic skin cleanser

colic A spasm of the bowel, usually seen in babies, with crying, irritability and drawing-up of knees.

comedone Medical label for what you and I call blackheads, as found in **acne**.

congenital A congenital skin blemish is one present at birth.

conjunctivitis An inflammation of the whites of the eyes, usually due to **allergy** or infection.

contractures With deep burns the skin heals as though it had 'shrunk'. There is thickening, hardening and shortening of the affected area.

cortisone A naturally occuring **hormone** which can be artificially manufactured. It is used in tablet, injection, inhaler, cream and ointment forms for various treatments, such as **asthma**, **eczema** and hay fever. Cortisone is also known as steroid.

coxsackie The name given to a specific virus involved in the condition **hand, foot and mouth disease.**

crust A scab-type formation found on inflamed skin.

cryosurgery Also called cryotherapy. The use of intense freezing to destroy unwanted tissues. The destroyed zone then separates under a natural healing process leaving a cosmetically acceptable area (see Appendix 3).

curettage A destructive surgical method of removing skin tissue. Under an anaesthetic a very sharp 'ice-cream' shaped scoop (called a *curette*) is used to lift out the diseased tissue. The resulting healing takes some time.

cyst A balloon-type swelling under the skin, full of **sebum.**

dermatologist A doctor specializing in skin disorders.

dermis One of the layers of normal skin.

dermatophytosis A long-winded label for a **fungus** infection of the skin.

dermatitis See **eczema.**

densensitization An allergy treatment plan where a series of injections is given to stimulate immunity against certain specific substances.

diabetes A condition where the body does not produce enough of the **hormone** insulin. This hormone controls our blood sugar levels and in diabetes this rises to quite high levels.

Diane A medication used in the treatment of acne in girls only. It contains an artificial **hormone** and the treatment coincidentally exerts a contraceptive effect.

dithranol A specific treatment for use in **psoriasis.**

Down's syndrome A genetic abnormality which means that children born with this condition are mentally handicapped (among other things); also known as *mongolism*.

ecchymosis A large bleeding under the surface of the skin. Technical name for **bruise.**

eczema An inflammation of the skin producing an itch, redness and weeping (also called dermatitis).

eczema herpeticum A dangerous complication of **eczema** where the herpes virus causes a spreading infection of the skin.

epidermis The outer protective layer of normal skin.

erythema Medical term for redness of the skin.

erythromycin One of a group of **antibiotics** used to treat infections caused by **bacteria.**

flexures The fronts of the elbows, backs of the knees and behind the ears.

follicle The root of the hair where all growth begins.

fungus See **ringworm.**

gentian violet A purple-coloured anti-fungal preparation often used to treat mouth and nappy **thrush** infection. It stains clothes and skin purple and takes some days to wear away.

guttate (psoriasis) A descriptive term for a type of **psoriasis** more often seen in children where the rash begins in a droplet formation.

Herpid The trade name for a preparation used to treat **herpes** skin infections.

Hismanal The trade name for a specific **antihistamine.**

hormones These are chemicals produced naturally in the body for specific functions; for example, insulin controls our blood-sugar levels. There are a large number of hormones, many of which can be manufactured artificially and used in treatment routines; for example, **cortisone** is used in treating **eczema.**

house dust mites Tiny insects that live in and feed off ordinary household dust. They are involved in many **allergy** problems by coming into direct contact with tissue when they circulate in the air.

hydrocortisone A mild form of **cortisone.**

inflammation A special response in the skin to various stimuli with redness, swelling, itching and weeping.

infestation The description for skin or hair invaded by various burrowing insects, as, for example, in **scabies.**

lesion A blanket term for any type of skin blemish.

lindane A specific treatment used in some forms of skin **infestation.**

macule A discoloration (usually red) of the skin, but not raised up on the surface.

malignant In medical parlance this is used to describe a condition which has turned cancerous.

moisturizer A simple, non-scented skin preparation used to help dry skin conditions. Moisturizers are also useful as 'barriers' in that they protect the underlying skin from irritation.

naevus A medical label for what you and I call a **mole.**

Nalcrom The trade name for a product widely used in food-**allergy** conditions.

nits A descriptive term for head-lice **infestation**, which refers to the visible egg-cases left by the lice.

nodule A localized thickening of the skin.

Opticrom The trade name for a product used in eye **allergies.**

paediatric dermatologist A doctor who specializes in children's skin problems.

papule An 'above-the-surface' discoloration of the skin, as occurs in *chicken-pox.*

pediculosis A general term for **infestation** of the skin or pubic area with burrowing insects.

pernicious anaemia A specific type of anaemia due to lack of vitamin B$_{12}$.

petechia (pl. *petechiae*) A small, pinpoint area of bleeding under the surface of the skin.

plasma When blood is broken down into its various constituents, the bulk is found to be a clear fluid called plasma.

polyp These are fleshy swellings inside the nose, which occur in very allergic children, producing symptoms such as blockage, snuffles and itch.

port-wine stain The common term for a purplish discoloration of the skin, present from birth, and which affects almost one-half of the face.

potassium permanganate A purple solution widely used to clean infected skin conditions. It stains skin, clothes and baths and so should be used with care.

pustule A blister containing pus, usually meaning an infection is present.

Regaine A trade name for a lotion used to treat baldness (not yet used in children).

retinoic acid A vitamin A derivative used as a skin preparation in acne.

rhinitis An inflammation of the inner lining of the nose, usually due to **allergy.**

ringworm A fungus infection of the skin.

Roaccutane A relatively new drug used in severe acne. It can only be prescribed by a skin specialist and must be monitored closely for signs of side-effects.

salicylic acid A common component of pastes and ointments, this can be used to treat scaly conditions of the skin. In stronger concentrations it is used to kill off warts.

sarcoptes The invading insect in **scabies.**

sebaceous glands Glands associated with hair roots that produce **sebum.**

sebum The white cheesy material found in **cysts** and some types of **acne.** When you squeeze a pimple the stuff that comes out is sebum.

staphylococcus A specific **bacterium** often involved in skin infections.

streptococcus A specific **bacterium** often involved in throat infections but which can also cause skin infections.

steroid Another name for **cortisone.**

tar One of the oldest forms of treatment for many skin preparations but especially **eczema** and **psoriasis.**

tartrazine An artificial colouring agent used in food processing and involved in many **allergic reactions** in children.

tetracyclines A group of oral **antibiotics** used in the treatment of acne.

tinea See **ringworm.**

Tymasil A spray used to kill off **house dust mites.**

ulcer A distinct breakdown in the skin surface leaving the underlying tissue constantly exposed and raw.

vaccinia A very serious complication of atopic **eczema** where the child is exposed to smallpox vaccination. The immunizing virus can spread quickly in eczematous skin, causing a life-threatening illness.

vesicle A small blister containing clear fluid.

viruses The 'bugs' responsible for such infections as **measles** and **chicken-pox.**

weal A localized swelling of the skin, usually white or pinkish-white with surrounding redness that looks like a blister but without bursting. A weal is the hallmark of **allergy.**

Zovirax The trade name for a very important drug used to treat **herpes** virus infections.

Useful Addresses

British Dietetic Association,
103 Daimler House,
Paradise St.,
Birmingham B1 2BJ.
Tel: 021-643 5483.

British Red Cross Society,
9 Grosvenor Crescent,
London SW1X JEJ.
Tel: 01-235 5454.
(run a beauty care and cosmetic camouflage service).

Eczema Society of Ireland,
c/o Mary Inglis,
Kilfenora,
Gordon Ave.,
Foxrock,
Co. Dublin.
Tel: 01-893243.

National Childbirth Trust,
9 Queensborough Terrace,
London W2.
Tel: 01-221 3833.

National Eczema Society,
Tavistock House North,
Tavistock Square,
London WC1 9SR.
Tel: 01-388 4097.

Psoriasis Association,
7 Milton St.,
Northampton,
NN2 7JG.
Tel: 0604 711129.

Appendix 9

Helpful Books to Read

David Atherton, *Your Child with Eczema*, Heineman Medical.

Paul Carson, *Coping Successfully with Your Hyperactive Child*, Sheldon Press.

Paul Carson, *Coping Successfully with Your Child's Asthma*, Sheldon Press.

Paul Carson, *How to Cope with Your Child's Allergies*, Sheldon Press.

Patricia Gilbert, *Common Childhood Illnesses*, Sheldon Press.

Penelope Leach, *Baby and Child*, Penguin.

Ronald Marks, *Psoriasis*, Martin Dunitz: Macdonald Optima.

Ronald Marks, *Acne*, Martin Dunitz: Macdonald Optima.

Rona McKie, *Eczema and Dermatitis* Martin Dunitz: Macdonald Optima.

Joan Neilson, *Baby Care – The First Year*, Sheldon Press.

Christine Orton, *Learning to Live with Skin Disorders*, Souvenir Press.

Doreen Trust, *Overcoming Disfigurement*, Thorsons.

Paul van Riel, *Acne*, Sheldon Press.

Index

Dr Paul Carson

COPING SUCCESSFULLY WITH
YOUR HYPERACTIVE CHILD

Give your child a fresh start!
All you need to know about an
exhausting problem, with the
latest ideas about diet and food
additives.
£2.95

HOW TO COPE WITH YOUR
CHILD'S ALLERGIES

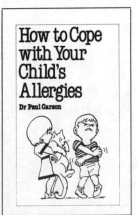

Help is at hand for hay-fever,
eczema and those mysterious
illnesses which leave your child
constantly under the weather.
With charts and checklists.
£2.95